Tall Buildings

wenig platz

gelbe hual

public
transportation

private
lift

rf. titanic
street

trusses

dec 02

Preface by Terence Riley   Essay by Guy Nordenson

Tall Buildings

The Museum of Modern Art, New York

This volume is published on the occasion of the exhibition
Tall Buildings, organized by Terence Riley, The Philip Johnson Chief
Curator of Architecture and Design, The Museum of Modern Art,
New York, and Guy Nordenson, Structural Engineer, New York City,
and Associate Professor of Architecture and Structures, Princeton
University, Princeton, New Jersey. The exhibition is on view at
MoMA QNS, July 16–September 27, 2004.

The exhibition is the second in a series of five made possible by
The Lily Auchincloss Fund for Contemporary Architecture.

The publication is made possible by Elise Jaffe and Jeffrey Brown.

The educational programs accompanying the exhibition are made
possible by BNP Paribas.

Produced by the Department of Publications,
The Museum of Modern Art, New York

Edited by Harriet Schoenholz Bee
Designed by Tsang Seymour Design, NY
Production by Christopher Zichello

Printed and bound by Dr. Cantz'sche Druckerei, Ostfildern, Germany
Typeset in TradeGothic and Grotesque
Printed on 150 gsm Zanders Mega matte

Library of Congress Control Number: 2003112777
ISBN: 0-87070-095-2

Published by The Museum of Modern Art,
11 West 53 Street, New York, New York 10019
(www.moma.org)
Distributed in the United States and Canada by
D.A.P./Distributed Art Publishers, Inc., New York
Distributed outside the United States and Canada
by Thames & Hudson, Ltd., London

Frontispiece: Renzo Piano (Renzo Piano Building Workshop) and
Ove Arup & Partners. London Bridge Tower, London, England.
Design 2000–03; projected completion, 2009. Sketch

Front cover: Norman Foster (Foster and Partners), Ysrael Seinuk and
Ahmad Rahimian (Cantor Seinuk Group). World Trade Center, New
York, New York. Project 2002. Model detail

Back cover: Rem Koolhaas and Ole Scheeren (Office for Metropolitan
Architecture), Cecil Balmond, Craig Gibbons, Michael Kwok, Rory
McGowan (Ove Arup & Partners). Central Chinese Television (CCTV)
Tower, Beijing, China. Design, 2002–04; projected completion,
2008. View from below (computer-generated image)

Front flap: William Pedersen (Kohn Pedersen Fox Associates),
George Chan (Ove Arup & Partners), Leslie Robertson (LERA).
Kowloon Station Tower, Hong Kong, China. Design, 2000–03;
projected completion, 2007. Section

Back flap: Adrian D. Smith and William F. Baker (Skidmore, Owings
& Merrill). 7 South Dearborn, Chicago, Illinois. Project, 1998.
Model

Printed in Germany

Contents

Foreword

In January 1933, a year after its landmark International Style exhibition, *Modern Architecture: International Exhibition,* The Museum of Modern Art launched its first show that included tall buildings: *Early Modern Architecture, Chicago, 1870–1910.* Organized by Henry-Russell Hitchcock and Philip Johnson, the exhibition celebrated the technical and aesthetic developments of the skyscraper. It included projects by the architects William Le Baron Jenney (who was also trained as an engineer), Henry Hobson Richardson, and Louis H. Sullivan, among others. The skyscraper was presented as "the most conspicuous achievement of American architecture in the second half of the nineteenth century."

Fifty years later, Arthur Drexler's exhibition *Three New Skyscrapers* celebrated similarly conspicuous achievements on an international scale, in Norman Foster's Hong Kong and Shanghai Bank, Hong Kong; Gordon Bunshaft's National Commercial Bank, Jedda; and Philip Johnson's and John Burgee's International Place at Fort Hill Square, Boston. In more recent years, *Ludwig Mies van der Rohe: Two Skyscrapers for Berlin* looked back to Mies's influential and, at the time, unrealizable idea of cladding an entire skyscraper in glass.

Bringing the Museum's interest in skyscrapers to the present, the twenty-five projects assembled for *Tall Buildings* by Terence Riley, The Philip Johnson Chief Curator of Architecture and Design, and Guy Nordenson, Structural Engineer, New York City, and Associate Professor of Architecture and Structures, Princeton University, Princeton, New Jersey, represent significant technological, aesthetic, and urbanistic transformations of the genre. Despite the formal, technical, and ecological complexities of these recent buildings, some of the themes in the present exhibition and catalogue echo such earlier concerns as the notion of the skeletal frame, discussed in 1931 in connection with William Le Baron Jenney's Home

Insurance Building, as being one of the defining features of tall buildings, or the idea of sheathing an entire skyscraper in glass, first proposed by Ludwig Mies van der Rohe in 1921. Today, the building skin—frequently entirely of glass—has become one of the tall building's defining features; increasingly, its surface plane directly manifests the ideas of sustainability, structural invention, and urban presence.

Early Modern Architecture, Chicago, which celebrated the period when the tall building came into being, followed the International Style exhibition, which featured four private houses that quickly became icons of modernism. It is fitting, therefore, that *Tall Buildings* should follow the *Un-Private House* as the second in a series of contemporary exhibitions sponsored by the Lily Auchincloss Fund for Contemporary Architecture. We are also grateful to Elise Jaffe and Jeffrey Brown for their support of the publication.

Finally, on the second anniversary of the World Trade Center disaster, which affected the lives of so many and brought the architectural discourse on tall buildings into the public realm, it is especially appropriate to address the pressing question of the reformulation of tall buildings, which continue to define our lives and contemporary cities. As *Tall Buildings* so clearly shows, architectural discussions of sustainability, safety, the extension of the city street, and aesthetic form can no longer been seen as solely the province of the architect as the artist-genius but must be reconceived as a true collaboration between architecture and structural engineering. I am most grateful to Terry Riley and Guy Nordenson for their joint creation of this important project and for bringing their insights on the most current developments in tall buildings to the fore.

Glenn D. Lowry
Director
The Museum of Modern Art

Preface

The construction of the World Trade Center towers in New York City, designed by the architect Minoru Yamasaki and the engineers John Skilling and Leslie Robertson, represented both a culmination and a hiatus in the development of tall buildings after World War II. When completed in 1973, the towers represented a substantial advance in the deployment of various technologies for high-rise design and construction, which had been developing over several decades. For the next fifteen years, the design of skyscrapers around the world was, with some notable exceptions, limited to trolling the waters in the enormous wake created by Yamasaki and Robertson. In other ways, the construction of the World Trade Center towers caused a feeling of disaffection with tall buildings. The sophisticated romance that had surrounded them earlier in the century had worn thin. In the postmodern mood of the day, the buildings were considered too tall. Proponents of traditional urban planning considered them not only out of scale with respect to the skyline but too disruptive at ground level.

Understandably, the swift destruction of the towers on September 11, 2001, provoked an intense scrutiny of tall buildings. Architects and engineers anxiously reconsidered their assumptions about structural soundness, emergency systems, and means of escape from office and residential towers. Politicians rendered opinions, some of them too hastily, on the complex building systems of the twin towers and made alternate proposals for making tall buildings terror proof. Former critics of the twin towers even suggested that we should not mourn their demise from an architectural or urban point of view. The general public, which had come to admire the twin towers, despite the disapproval of some architects, was nonetheless haunted by the images of their destruction.

As the heated initial debates on tall buildings subsided into more thoughtful and determined study, it became apparent that a reappraisal of tall buildings was not only appropriate and timely but also a bit overdue. Indeed, seminal projects such as the tower for the Hong Kong and Shanghai Bank, in Hong Kong, and the Commerzbank Headquarters, in Frankfurt, both designed by Norman Foster and Ove Arup & Partners; the Tour sans Fin, in Paris, designed by Jean Nouvel and Ove Arup & Partners; and the Bank of China, in

Hong Kong, designed by I.M. Pei and Leslie Robertson, demonstrated that, toward the late 1980s, a new generation of innovative skyscrapers was being developed around the globe, if not in Manhattan and Chicago, the tall building's traditional testing grounds.

This publication and the exhibition it accompanies focus on twenty-five tall buildings. They were designed within the last decade for sites around the world by an international group of architects and engineers. In selecting them, we have considered three fundamental aspects of the tall building: technology, urbanism, and program.

One of the principal drivers of innovation in skyscraper design continues to be technology. In terms of structure, some of the most remarkable recent advances have come through the use of sophisticated computer modeling, making the analysis and design of complex structural systems—within the compressed time frame of a building project—practical for the first time. The expansion of the engineer's analytical capabilities has produced a notable and effective enhancement of his or her role in collaborating in the design of tall buildings, with quite remarkable results. In this regard, the first realizations of diagonally braced structural skins are, perhaps, the most notable innovations in recent tall buildings. Whereas tall buildings previously were conceived as, or at least appeared to be, orthogonal matrices of vertical columns and horizontal slabs, a number of recent structures can be seen as freely composed rigid exterior skins, and even three-dimensional space frames, with correspondingly open interior spaces.

Another aspect of technological innovation in recent tall buildings is the design of structures that consume less energy than conventional ones. In the recent era of cheap energy and reduced consciousness about the environment, tall buildings, with millions of square feet, can be designed with ever-greater mechanical systems for cooling and heating, and with little concern for their collateral effects. Nevertheless, principally owing to tough European laws concerning energy efficiency and buttressed by individual concern about the environment, engineers and architects are, once again, using sophisticated computer analysis to reduce dependency on mechanical systems in tall buildings. The innovative use of double glazing to reduce solar gain, strategies for passive air flow within structures, improved computer modeling of air flow around buildings, and a host of other smaller but effective measures mean that recent tall buildings are demonstrably more efficient than the previous generation of high-rise construction.

Not surprisingly, the various towers proposed for the site of the World Trade Center focused on safety, and no doubt many of the innovations suggested will be adopted elsewhere. Enhanced emergency escape routes, more areas of refuge and means of rescue, and redundant systems of fire suppression and communication are sure to become the next areas in which regulation will be standardized.

While these and other important technological advances, such as earthquake damping and "smart" construction, are less evident, the scale of tall buildings guarantees that they will continue to define the contemporary metropolis. If the familiar appeal of skyscrapers has waned in urban places where they are ubiquitous, such as New York, the same cannot be said of cities around the world that are experiencing bursts of high-rise construction, such as Singapore. The sudden appearance of tall buildings on the skyline, morphing the identity of the urban landscape, expands the dimensions of a city, often making it a presence far beyond its traditional boundaries. Perhaps the most notable development in the use of tall buildings to make urban space is the adoption of alternate models to the tower, the tapering shaft rising like a column to the sky. Linked buildings, Möbius-like constructions, and other previously unseen forms not only act as defining markers but also create vast spaces and channel vision over great dimensions. In cities that are already dominated by high-rise skylines, more mature visions of the tall building as one of an ensemble are also evident, creating interrelationships that also mitigate the concept of the tall building as an isolated tower.

Another urban feature of the tall building that continues to develop is the "city within the city," first used to describe the heterogeneous program of Rockefeller Center's cluster of tall buildings in midtown Manhattan. Many contemporary tall buildings are conceived to expand and magnify the public domain, and are thus more permeable and transparent. Greater attention is being paid to the life of the city at ground level, whether it is pedestrian circulation, public space, or commercial activity, than to establishing towers in plazas. Previously, rather formal and forbidding lobbies designated the line between public activity at grade and private space above; now many recent tall buildings also seek to extend the activities of the street into the structure, not least of all by locating the structures above existing transportation centers and linking the tall buildings with local and regional transport.

It is, perhaps, in this last respect that architects around the world are resisting the common wisdom in a post–September 11 world: reduce the public sphere, restrict access, and limit unmonitored activity. Despite anxieties of a changed global environment, architects today recognize that the tall building can never be separated from the permeable fabric of the city and from the public activity from which it grows.

Terence Riley
The Philip Johnson Chief Curator
of Architecture and Design
The Museum of Modern Art, New York

Tall Building as Metaphor

By Guy Nordenson

The "tall buildings," which have ... usurped a glory that affects you as rather surprised, ... the multitudinous sky-scrapers standing up to the view, from the water, like extravagant pins in a cushion already overplanted, and stuck in as in the dark, anywhere and anyhow, have at least the felicity ... of taking the sun and the shade in the manner of towers of marble. They are not all of marble, I believe, by any means, even if some may be, but they are impudently new and still more impudently "novel"—this in common with so many other terrible things in America—and they are triumphant payers of dividends; all of which, with flash of innumerable windows and flicker of subordinate gilt attributions, is like the flare, ... of the lamps of some general permanent "celebration."
—Henry James, 1906 [1]

After the terrorist attacks on New York and Washington on September 11, 2001, it was natural to wonder why the World Trade Center towers and not the Statue of Liberty had been the target in New York, why Al Quaeda had chosen a symbol of commerce over a symbol of freedom.[2] Whatever the answer, there is little doubt that if it had been attacked, the statue would have been rebuilt (as was the Pentagon) and not replaced (as the World

Trade Center will be). What is not as clear is how it would have been rebuilt, and what that would have meant.

Tall buildings, if only by being tall, look to stand out in a crowd. In time they may become the crowd, but it is always their intention to speak up, to declare, indeed, even persuade us of their novelty, their sumptuousness, their responsibility to social needs and ideals, their outright beauty, and their abstraction. The World Trade Center towers were built to revitalize downtown Manhattan, and promote globalization. Like Rockefeller Center, they expressed a unique moment of civic will. And they became exponents of global commerce in the marketplace of New York City. After their destruction, the same expression of civic will did not re-emerge; what did emerge was more of our own time.

The Statue of Liberty has always remained, in its solitude, the clearest voice in that marketplace of ideas, in the agora not just of the city but at large: it stands for liberty. And it stands, in fact, because of a particular set of circumstances, ideals, talents, and resources that brought it into being. But its meaning is such that, long after all these particularities have been forgotten, it could never have been a target on September 11. This

FIG. 1. Frédéric-Auguste Bartholdi, Alexandre-Gustave Eiffel, and Richard Morris Hunt. Statue of Liberty. 1881–84

may tell us how we might begin to understand the meaning of the tall building or structure. Each is an expression, a "speech act" in the agora. And each is constituted, of necessity, not by a single artist's hand but by the condensation of events and individual talents. Thus, each becomes a metaphor.

Originally intended as a gift of the French nation to the United States on the centenary of the Declaration of Independence, the Statue of Liberty was the idea of a group of republican gentlemen and businessmen led by the journalist and politician Édouard-René Lefebvre de Laboulaye, who also hoped to promote the principles of *liberté, égalité, fraternité* at home in France.[3] The enterprise was conceived near Versailles in 1865, the year of Abraham Lincoln's assassination, and came of age in 1871, the year of the Paris Commune. The French sculptor Frédéric-Auguste Bartholdi was commissioned to create the statue, which he derived from an amalgam of allegorical and other sources, notably the traditional figures of Faith and Truth,[4] the great *colossi* of Thebes in Egypt, and even Eugène Delacroix's heroic canvas, *Liberty Guiding the People* of 1830. The French architect, engineer, and critic Eugène-Emmanuel Viollet-le-Duc was asked to undertake its structural design, but died in 1879 before it could be completed. He was succeeded by the French engineer Alexandre-Gustave Eiffel, whose landmark tower in Paris—at 984 feet (300 meters) the tallest man-made structure of the time—was erected ten years later in 1889. Surprisingly, Eiffel does not appear to have shown much interest in his work on the Statue of Liberty (page 10), and described it as designed according to "the conditions of strict economy which circumstances imposed," designing "an iron framework which would serve as a support for the whole of the copper envelope," and would form "a sort of large pylon secured at four points to the masonry base supporting the statue."[5] Eiffel's contribution, however invisible at first, subtly deepens the statue's meaning. Much of its presence and power can be attributed to its colossal scale, its almost still stance, its vast interior and paper-thin copper "skin," its sophisticated structural order of trussed spine, light outriggers, and the delicate springs and bars holding the skin,

the radical pre-tensioned cable system anchoring the statue to the pedestal, and finally the beautifully composed pedestal evoking the great stone past, from Egypt to France, which frames the light and lightness above. Eiffel was undoubtedly the greatest engineer of his day. His contribution, perhaps more than those of his colleagues, does a great deal in raising the work to its iconic status.

The Statue of Liberty was the project of three men who worked independently: the sculpture by Bartholdi, the structure by Eiffel, and the pedestal by the American architect Richard Morris Hunt. Each man's work was attentive and sensitive to that of the others, and the work emerged with a sublime resonance of its own (Fig. 1). Even after over a hundred years, the Statue of Liberty can still serve as an interpretive example of the well-made tall building, one that might be thought of as an ideogram of form, structure, program, symbol, and fabrication, as the product of a strong collaborative process, and as a "speech act" in the urban marketplace.

If the statue were ever reconstructed, it might be rebuilt in a number of ways. One possible model might be the Solomon R. Guggenheim Museum in Bilbao, Spain (1991–97), by the American architect Frank O. Gehry—like the statue, a large-scale sculptural object, powerful urban intervention, complex interior space, and individualized structure. Yet, a comparison of sections (cross sections) of the statue and the Bilbao museum (Figs. 2, 3), makes it apparent how they differ structurally: the latter is dialectical, the former monolithic. Gehry's building is in the tradition of early expressionistic architecture (by Erich Mendelsohn and Hans Poelzig, for example) and also of the later, more technological, expressionistic works by Jørn Utzon and Eero Saarinen.[6] In Utzon's Sydney Opera House (1956–74) the architect and the structural engineers Ove Arup and Jack Zunz created, in close collaboration, parallel achievements of form and structure, each distinct and legible (Fig. 4).[7] Similarly, Saarinen's collaboration with the engineer Fred Severud on the St. Louis Arch (1965) and with engineers Paul Weidlinger and Mario Salvadori on the CBS Building (1961–65) are instances of highly inventive structural engineering contained by and directed toward a formal objective (Fig. 5).

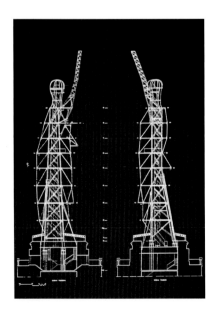

FIG. 2. Sections of the Statue of Liberty, 1986; drawing by Swanke Hayden Connell Architects

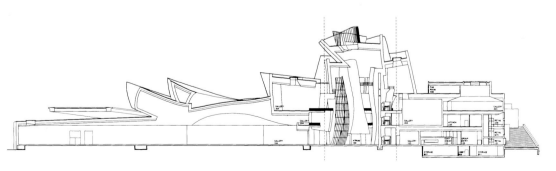

FIG. 3. Frank O. Gehry. Longitudinal section of the Solomon R. Guggenheim Museum in Bilbao, Spain, 1991–97

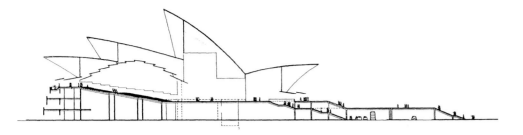

FIG. 4. Jørn Utzon and Ove Arup & Partners. Longitudinal section of the Sydney Opera House, Sydney, Australia, 1956–74

FIG. 6. Bruce Graham and Fazlur Khan, Skidmore, Owings & Merrill. Sears Tower, Chicago, 1970–74

In contrast, such tall buildings as the Sears Tower in Chicago (1970–74) by Bruce Graham and Fazlur Khan of Skidmore, Owings & Merrill (Fig. 6) and the World Trade Center towers in New York (1966–73) by Minoru Yamasaki and the engineers Leslie Robertson and John Skilling more fully integrate structure and form (Fig. 7). This is largely because of the extreme demands of their scale but also because they were conceived at the outset as expressing the means and wonder of their structural art and achievement.

These are differences of kind, not of quality or effectiveness. One kind of work (the dialectical) holds the technological and architectural meaning apart, allowing the meaning to emerge gradually, while the other approach (the monolithic) aims to fully integrate them in an organic whole. An example of the former, in another discipline, might be that of the Russian filmmaker Sergei Eisenstein, who developed a theory of sound and moving pictures that proposed the conjuncture of sound and image (and, for that matter, image and image—montage) as a means to "give birth to the image in which the thematic matter is most clearly embodied."[8] He even suggested a kind of narrative space with pictures in the horizontal and sound in the vertical, in effect, a kind of space structure.[9] He referred to the American orientalist and educator

Ernest Fenollosa's *The Chinese Written Character as a Medium for Poetry.*[10] Fenollosa and his translator, Ezra Pound, argued that such juxtapositions made meaning and could make it new. Taking their inspiration from the visual construction of Chinese written characters or ideograms—and the way they apparently construct meaning through metaphoric relations—Fenollosa and Pound stated: "Relations are more real and more important than the things they relate. The forces which produce the branch-angles of an oak lay potent in the acorn. Similar lines of resistance, half-curbing the out-pressing vitalities, govern the branching of rivers and of nations. Thus a nerve, a wire, a roadway, and a clearing house are only varying channels which communication forces for itself. This is more than analogy, it is identity of structure."[11]

In 1914 Pound introduced his idea of the *vortex* as "a radiant node or cluster … from which, and through which, and into which, ideas are constantly rushing."[12] In architecture, he pointed to the Tempio Malatestiano in Rimini (1446–68) to illustrate the vortex (Fig. 8). There, works by the architect Leon Battista Alberti, the painter Piero della Francesca, the sculptor Agostino di Duccio, and the Lombardi brothers, an architect and a sculptor, are conjoined with a preexisting church, San Francesco of Rimini, and together celebrate the achievement of its patron, the ruthless *condottiere* Sigismondo Malatesta. It is a confluence of disparate energy that weaves a cohesive and lasting pattern.

FIG. 7. View of the World Trade Center and the Statue of Liberty from New York harbor

FIG. 5. Eero Saarinen, Paul Weidlinger, and Mario Salvadori. Aerial view of the CBS Building, New York, under construction, 1961–65

FIG. 8. Tempio Malatestiano, Rimini, Italy, 1446–68

FRAME CRAFT

Eiffel took over the structural engineering of the Statue of Liberty in 1879, the design was completed around 1880, and the statue first erected in Paris in 1881–84. In Chicago, at the outset of tall-building architecture, the first complete steel-frame structure, the Home Insurance Building (1884–85), was constructed by the architect William Le Baron Jenney and the engineer George B. Whitney. Vertical trusses were first used, as wind bracing, on the twenty-two-story Masonic Temple (1891–92) in Chicago by Daniel Burnham and John Wellborn Root, as well as on the Unity Building of the same year by Clinton Warren (Fig. 9).

In some cases, Chicago architects, particularly in the mid-1890s, were able to reduce the visible presence of the steel frame almost completely. For instance, in the Reliance Building (1890–95) by Charles Atwood of Burnham and Company, the terracotta and glass facade weaves back and forth, hiding evidence of columns in the folds of the bay windows and corners, and becoming a true curtain wall (Fig. 10). But these cases were uncommon. More often, as in the Gage Group (1898) by William Holabird and Martin Roche and the adjacent 18 South Michigan Avenue (1898–99) by Louis Sullivan, the frame was clearly expressed as slender masonry piers and spandrels around the classic Chicago tripartite window (Fig. 11). Starting with the First Leiter Building (1879) by Jenney (which still had load-bearing masonry piers), continuing to Louis Sullivan's Carson Pirie Scott Store (1899, 1903–04, 1906), and well into the 1900s this gave a clear and direct reading of the structural frame, from top to bottom.

The key exceptions to this are Dankmar Adler's and Louis Sullivan's Wainwright Building in St. Louis (1890–91) and their Guaranty Building in Buffalo (1894–95) (Fig. 12). Both are classical compositions in the vertical and horizontal, with the distinct base, shaft, and top advocated by Sullivan, with massive piers anchoring the corners, and uniform vertical masonry piers across the facade. The actual difference between the structural and nonstructural facade piers is obscured by their equivalent appearance.[13]

Here, at the birth of the skyscraper, we can see the distinction between direct and veiled structural expression. The Reliance, Wainwright, and Guaranty buildings allow a reading of the structure but not without some ambiguity between the primary load-bearing and secondary facade-framing structures. Atwood as well as Adler and Sullivan also sought to veil or blend these in order to express an organic and bounded whole,[14] whereas the more conventional Chicago School facades are grids of potentially infinite extension.

In his essay "Chicago Frame," the late British architectural historian Colin Rowe argued that when the European architects adopted the frame, it was as a polemical device and counterpoint to space making.[15] The Chicago architects were not, on the other hand, that interested in shaping space. And their successor Frank Lloyd Wright chose not to use the frame for his few tall building proposals, but, rather, adopted something like Eiffel's spine and outrigger (or tree-and-branch) structure for his Saint Mark's Tower (1929), which was later built as the Price Tower in 1956. In doing so he transformed the organic idea of his mentor Louis Sullivan from the outside into the plan,

FIG. 9. Clinton Warren. Unity Building, Chicago, 1891–92

FIG. 10. Charles Atwood, Burnham and Company. Reliance Building, Chicago, 1890–95

FIG. 11. LEFT TO RIGHT William Holabird and Martin Roche. Gage Group, 30 and 24 South Michigan Avenue, 1898; Louis H. Sullivan. 18 South Michigan Avenue, Chicago, 1898–99

FIG. 12. Dankmar Adler and Louis H. Sullivan. Guaranty Building, Buffalo, 1894–95

using the core as the center of his whirling spaces.

While Eiffel's graphical calculations for the Statue of Liberty show a clear understanding of the effect of wind load on the structure, at that time nothing was required by the New York City building code for structures up to one hundred feet with respect to wind load.[16] The code simply specified an increase in the thickness of masonry walls as height increased. Many early New York skyscrapers were built as so-called cage constructions, with self-supporting exterior walls tied back to complete steel or iron frames. Other early towers were erected with load-bearing masonry. This method resembles that used in the construction of Venetian palazzos, a cage wrapped in a veneer, but at a much larger scale and with frames of steel, not wood. This may be said to reflect the similar emphasis in both mercantile cultures on the confectionary—on a stage set and not a curtain.

In 1906, the architect Cass Gilbert started his 90 West Street Building (1906–07) in New York, which was a precursor to his later design for the great Woolworth Building (1910–13) (Fig. 13). Also in 1906, Stanford White was shot in his Madison Square Garden Building of 1889–90, and Philip Johnson was born. In New York, skyscrapers have typically been more like towers than tall buildings, and they are often quite slender and stylistically derivative. The Madison Square Garden tower, for instance, was an enlarged copy of the Giralda of the Cathedral of Seville. Other buildings are inflations of the Italian campanile, and still others, like the Woolworth Building, are derived from French Gothic cathedral bell towers. Johnson's later buildings in New York, the former AT&T Headquarters (1984) and the so-called Lipstick Building (1986), perpetuated that tradition.

Generally, New York skyscrapers, in both concept and construction, divided the exterior expression and interior make-up. The cage and, later, curtain-wall constructions were taken up by New York architects as occasions to develop formal languages that were usually independent of the interior spatial, structural, or servicing realities of their buildings. This differs from both Venetian and Chicago practice. In Venice, the elaborate gothic facades of the Ca D'Oro (1421–40) and the Ducal Palace (1465–79) are at the same time patterned surfaces and an articulate expression of interior spatial arrangements and meanings.[17] They are examples of what the British critic and painter Adrian Stokes has described as: "Such artificiality in astonishing unity with such realism … where nature in exotic form conspires with good sense."[18] It was the disjunction of content and surface in New York skyscrapers, that caused Henry James to write: "Crowned not only with no history, but with no credible possibility of time for history, and consecrated by no uses save the commercial at any cost, they are simply the most piercing notes in that concert of the expensively provisional into which your supreme sense of New York resolves itself."[19]

Comparing New York structures, such as the Woolworth Building, to Chicago's Reliance Building, it is obvious that most New York architects and engineers went about their work separately, with little concern for harmony or metaphoric resonance. Another way to understand this is to examine the work of the partners Charles McKim and Stanford White. McKim was responsible for bringing the Guastavino masons to the United States to work on his Boston Library, and designed the Low Library dome at Columbia University (1893–1903) as a load-bearing masonry shell. White built the Gould Library at New York University's Bronx campus of steel trusses clad in stone and plaster. McKim took care to include careful craft in the execution of his work, while White, the man about town, cared mainly for the appearance. McKim had studied closely the architecture and construction methods of the Romans and understood that style was tied to craft, even when transmuted through abstraction.

Louis Sullivan wrote in *Kindergarten Chats* that his function as an architect was: "to vitalize building materials, to animate them collectively with a thought, a state of feeling, to charge them with a subjective significance and value, to make them visible parts of the genuine social fabric, to infuse into them the true life of the people, to impart to them the best that is in the people, as the eye of the poet, looking below the surface of life, sees the best that is in the people."[20] William Le Baron Jenney wrote in 1891: "There must be sufficient material and no more, for it is essential, not only for economy but also to reduce the weights on the foundations, that the construction should be as light as possible consistent with stability."[21] In Chicago, designers of tall buildings were constrained by the unstable soil conditions to take particular care in the design of their foundations and to keep the buildings light. In New York, the hard bedrock both downtown and in midtown made greater whimsy possible. Only instances such as the Statue of Liberty, which had to be built light for transport from Paris to New York, or the now-demolished, slender forty-seven-story Singer Tower (1906–08) by Ernest Flagg (Fig. 14), required well-conceived structures that then could contribute something to the meaning of the buildings.

CITIZEN SKYSCRAPER

After the Woolworth Building and the changes in the New York City building and zoning code of 1916 (which resulted from the construction of the massive Equitable Building in 1912–16), things were calm for a time. In Chicago, the creative energy of the 1890s had shifted to the residential work of the Prairie School, and the remarkable

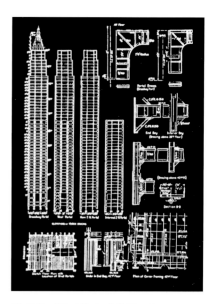

FIG. 13. Cass Gilbert. Woolworth Building, New York, 1910–13. Elevations, plan, and structural details

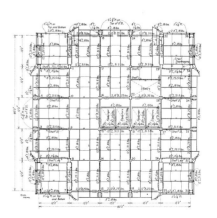

FIG. 14. Ernest Flagg. Singer Tower, New York, 1906–08. Typical floor framing plan

FIG. 15. Eliel Saarinen. Grand Hotel, Chicago, Project 1923. Perspective drawing

plastic and planimetric inventions of Frank Lloyd Wright. As the Italian historian Manfredo Tafuri has demonstrated in his essay "The Disenchanted Mountain," it was the Chicago Tribune Competition and exhibition of 1922 that brought together all the strange and remarkable strands that had evolved from the Chicago and New York skyscrapers. On the one hand, there was the "anarchic individual," and on the other, there were those making buildings that "had first and foremost to convey a composite significance."[22] In a discussion of the Chicago Tribune entry by Eliel Saarinen, Tafuri wrote: "His interpretation of the skyscraper is, in fact, exactly the opposite of the whole American experience in the matter of the skyscraper: not a structure materializing the concept of laissez-faire, and thus not an image of the competition among the great commercial concentrations but an element capable of exercising a formal control over the urban complex as a whole."[23] In a subsequent project for the Grand Hotel and the Chicago lakefront (1923) (Fig. 15), Eliel Saarinen extended this idea and contributed a remarkable plan that foreshadowed the nine-square plan of the Sears Tower.

As eclectic, or anarchic, as were the separate designs for the Chicago Tribune competition, none demonstrated the weaving of "patterned energies" of structure, symbol, space, and form that exists at the Statue of Liberty or even the Reliance Building. The entry that came the closest to this was the Adolf Meyer and Walter Gropius design (Fig. 16), a careful composite of structural expression, expressive facade articulation, skilled asymmetric massing, and memorable rendering from a three-quarter perspective. Tafuri clearly described the transformation of the type, from skyscraper to a kind of "literary image." On the work of Hugh Ferris, including the Metropolis of Tomorrow (1929), Tafuri offered the following judgment: "The historical significance of the designs of this able conjurer of images lies in their poetic celebration of the skyscraper. The skyscraper is 'sung' by Ferris in an attempt to restore an 'enchantment' to what could by this time be only a 'disenchanted mountain.' In this sense Ferris was Saarinen's only follower in the 1920s, and with reason; only as a purely literary image could the skyscraper any longer assume an 'aura.' The results of the *Chicago Tribune* competition had made this quite clear."[24]

Tafuri's mention of Ferris having "sung" the skyscraper, was an obvious reference to Walt Whitman's "I Sing the Body Electric" from *Leaves of Grass* (1855) where the American poet wrote:

But the expression of a well-made man
appears not only in his face,
It is in his limbs and joints also, it is curiously
in the joints of his hips and wrists,
It is in his walk, the carriage of his neck,
the flex of his waist and knees,
dress does not hide him,
The strong sweet quality he has strikes
through the cotton and broadcloth;
To see him pass conveys as much as the best
poem, perhaps more,
You linger to see his back, and the back of
his neck and shoulder-side.[25]

Here is the idea of a complete and self-generated whole, something new, synthetic: a vortex, in Pound's sense of the word.

The very diversity of kind and quality manifest in the Chicago Tribune Competition dissipated any notion of the city as a whole. The great tall buildings constructed between the wars in New York— Raymond Hood's Daily News and McGraw-Hill buildings (1930–31), William Van Alen's Chrysler Building (1930), and Shreve, Lamb and Harmon's Empire State Building (1931)—were strong individual objects, both self-publicizing and acquiescent to market needs. The structure of the city, the structure of the real-estate business, the structure of the construction industry, the structure of the buildings—all were unaffected by the conceptual work of design. The design styles did vary—the Daily News and McGraw-Hill buildings, built only a year apart on opposite ends of Forty-second Street, had opposite formal emphases but equally ad-hoc means of construction. The massing and facades are quite different, but all else is the same.

FIG. 16. Adolf Meyer and Walter Gropius, Chicago Tribune Competition Entry, Project 1922. Model

Even the Empire State Building, although constructed at breakneck speed (eighty-five stories in six months) and with great inventiveness by the Starrett Brothers and Eken,[26] had little to contribute to advance the arts of architecture or engineering. It does not convey the thrill of Whitman's "well-made man." The structure for the Empire State Building was designed by Homer G. Balcom for speed of erection, not lightness. With 57,480 tons of steel for 2.1 million square feet, it required about fity pounds per square foot of structural steel to reach its 1,252-foot height.[27] Balcom was also the engineer of the buildings at Rockefeller Center (1931–40). His design for the former RCA Building (1931–33), in particular, is noteworthy for the fact that in the narrow direction it uses diagonal braces to resist the wind forces, but on the broad north and south facades, in the other direction, it relies, as does the Empire State Building, on the interaction of the riveted-steel frame with the brick masonry and stone cladding filling in that frame to resist the wind (Fig. 17). This represents a rather typical hybrid usage of "nonstructural" cladding masonry to resist wind load, characteristic of the continued ad-hoc approach of New York architects and structural engineers when it comes to the means and materials of building.[28]

While Rockefeller Center may have neither the structural elegance of the Statue of Liberty nor the closely choreographed construction speed of the Empire State Building, it is of fundamental significance as a sterling instance of ensemble design and urban power. For Le Corbusier: "Rockefeller Center affirms to the world the dignity of the new times [and] the proclamation of a proper name, that of a financial success, a fortune a monetary power. Thus in the Middle Ages, at San Gimignano in Tuscany, the struggles for control among the families of the little city brought about the construction of fantastically high towers.... San Gimignano has the appearance of a pin cushion, and the spectacle delights tourists while troubling common sense; hirsute beauty—yes beauty, why not? The cataclysms of nature—jagged rocks,

Niagara, Alps, or canyons, do they not impel our admiration by the effect of power, the feeling of catastrophe?"[29] For Tafuri: "Rockefeller Center ... represented the final result of the general debate on the structure of the American city.... It demonstrated that the only type of undertaking with any real possibility of influencing urban dynamics was one limited in scale and wholly in keeping with the existing, traditional laws of urban growth.... Indeed, if Rockefeller Center contained any ideological residue, it was in this attempt to celebrate the reconciliation of the trusts and the collectivity on an urban scale.... Rockefeller Center marked the definite eclipse of the 'skyscraper as an individual.' Presenting itself as 'a city within a city,' it had no need to create shock effects, as did the McGraw-Hill, Daily News, or Chrysler buildings."[30]

Both Le Corbusier and Tafuri recognized the necessarily composite meaning of tall buildings, understood them as urban in scale but suggestive, as well, of a way for design practice to create individual buildings. The best works, from the unintentional composite brilliance of the Statue of Liberty, the Reliance Building, and even the Monadnock Block (1889–91) (Fig. 18),[31] all the way to Le Corbusier's astonishing Cartesian Skyscraper (1935) and Obus E Project for Algiers (1939) (Fig. 19), are at least careful compositions of space, fabric, structure, and form. It is possible to find an equilibrium of forms among the rhetorical and real aspects of formal language and technological content, where neither one is diminished nor dominant. A classical language need not dress up a banal interior, nor must a technological imperative determine the total integration of the whole. Instead, a conjunction of forces can flow in a "patterned energy," or vortex.

FIG. 17. Shreve, Lamb and Harmon. Empire State Building, New York, under construction, 1931

FIG. 19. Le Corbusier. Obus E Project for Algiers, Algeria, 1939. Model

RHETORIC, POETRY, AND ART

John Wellborn Root, the architect of the Monad-nock Block, and, incidentally, the brother-in-law of the founder of *Poetry* magazine, Harriet Monroe, wrote in 1890: "Like all forms of civilization, architectural development has for centuries moved from homogeneity to heterogeneity … to be true, architecture must normally express the conditions of life about and within it, not in a fragmentary and spasmodic way, but in the mass and structure; the life of the building, in large and comprehensive type."[32]

This means incorporating the facts of the "age of steam, of electricity, of gas, of plumbing and sanitation" into a "new art, a rational and steady growth from practical conditions outward and upward toward a more or less spiritual expression."[33] According to the architect and critic Alan Colquhoun, in "Pax Americana," a chapter in his *Modern Architecture* (2002): "Perhaps the greatest single achievement of American architecture after the Second World War was the establishment of the modern corporate office building as a type, imitated all over the world."[34]

In the United States, Lever House (1950–52) and the Inland Steel Building (1956–57) by Skidmore, Owings & Merrill, and the Seagram Building (1954–58) by Ludwig Mies van der Rohe; in Brazil, the Ministry of Education and Health Building in Rio de Janeiro (1936–43) by Lucio Costa, Oscar Niemeyer, and others (with Le Corbusier consulting)—were retranslations from Europe of earlier American frame buildings, through abstraction and free planning. The originals ranged from Mies van der Rohe's Glass Skyscraper (1921), the Chicago Tribune Building proposals (1922) of Meyer and Gropius and Ludwig Hilberseimer, and Le Corbusier's Cartesian Skyscraper and Algiers project to the various speculations of the Vesnin brothers and Ivan Leonidov in 1920s Russia. As Colin Rowe wrote: "A formula was evolved permitting the simultaneous appearance of both structural grid and considerable spatial complexity…. In the International Style an autonomous structure perforates a freely abstracted space, acting as its punctuation rather than its defining form. There is thus … no fusion of space and structure, but each in the end remains an identifiable component, and architecture is conceived, not as their confluence, but rather as their dialectical opposition, as a species of debate between them."[35] For example, with the Lever House the opposing bodies of vertical and horizontal prisms float beside and bracket a cubic negative space (Fig. 20). The columns are sharply detailed stainless-steel cladding and are clearly separate from the tightly wrapped fabric of glass and stainless-steel vertical mullions. Prior to the recent restoration, the facade was even more remarkable

FIG. 20. Gordon Bunshaft, Skidmore, Owings & Merrill, and Weiskopf & Pickworth. Lever House, New York, 1950–52

for its variation in spandrel-panel glass color, from light marine blue to indigo, a subtle counterpoint to the building's machined and prismatic appearance.[36] And, like the Inland Steel Building, the building also clearly segregates office space and a core or service zone.

It is instructive to compare the plan of the former RCA Building at Rockefeller Center (1930–33) (Fig. 21) and that of the Chase Manhattan Bank Headquarters (1957–61) by Gordon Bunshaft (Fig. 22), the architect of Lever House. Both are commissions of the Rockefeller family, although a generation apart. The most significant difference seems to be that the RCA Building has been composed as a volume from the outside in— a contingent object clearly fitted to its protagonist role at the urban scale—while the Chase building is also composed in plan, with emphasis on the column-free spans. The idea of the open space without columns is an important generator of the Chase design. The columns are expressed in the exterior as stainless-steel clad pilasters all the way up and down. Their presence on the facade suggests an open light-filled space within. The buildings of the 1920s and 1930s on the other hand, from Rockefeller Center to the Empire State Building, did not suggest that the interior spaces were likely to be all that open or pleasant.

The use of glass plays a crucial role in this context. The glass curtain wall, despite the occasional successes of the 1890s, did not gain a firm hold until the post–World War II period. Glass offers lightness, transparency, and reflection, and the allusion to crystals.[37] An interesting precursor to some of the late modern crystal-like building forms is Wenzel Hablik's 1920 Exhibition Building (Fig. 23). It is unusual in that it prescribes both a sculpturally strong form (almost like an Easter Island figure) and a completely regular and rationalized structure of load-bearing vertices, anticipating the later investigations of Myron Goldsmith and of I. M. Pei.

The ambition has changed since Root argued that: "Looking at the problems presented by these buildings … we may certainly guess that all pre-existing architectural forms are inadequate for their solution."[38] But to Root and the American architects that followed: "Styles are found truly at the appointed time, but solely by those who, with intelligence and soberness, are working their ends by the best means at hand, and with scarce a thought of the coming new or natural style … if the new art is to come, I believe it will be a rational and steady growth from practical conditions outward and upward toward a more or less spiritual expression."[39] This argues, as Montgomery Schuyler wrote, that expression is an organic manifestation of the "true nature" of the thing, the building—"as it must be."[40] But this of course implies ambiguity, in that it is not just as it must be but as the society would have it be: "normal." In a 1964 text, *La Tour Eiffel*, Roland Barthes counters what he regards as pseudo-arguments for utility—the tower as meteorological or other scientific platform, or as a site for high-altitude medical research: "Here the utilitarian reasons, as ennobled as they might be by the myth of Science, are nothing in comparison to the imagination which, alone, serves men to be properly human. Nevertheless, as ever, the gratuitous meaning of the work is not always admitted directly; it is rationalized by usage."[41] To Barthes: "Architecture is always dream and function, the expression of a utopia and the instrument of comfort."[42]

The Anglo-Welsh Roman Catholic poet and critic David Jones, who died in 1974, wrote in a 1947 essay, "Art and Democracy," of the "gratuitous which is the *sine qua non* of art…. If we could catch the beaver placing never so small a twig *gratuitously* we could make his dam into a font, he would be patient of baptism—the whole 'sign-world' would be open to him, he would know 'sacrament' and would have a true culture, for a culture is nothing but a sign, and the *anathemata* of a culture, 'the things set up,' can be set up only

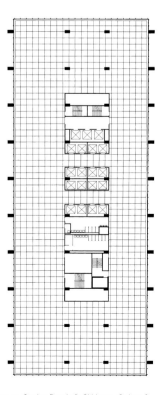

FIG. 22. Gordon Bunshaft, Skidmore, Owings & Merrill, and Weiskopf & Pickworth. Chase Manhattan Bank Building, New York, 1957–61. Typical floor plan (tower)

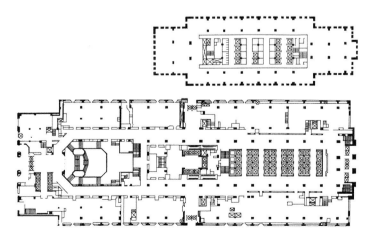

FIG. 21. Raymond Hood. RCA Building at Rockefeller Center (now the GE Building), New York, 1931–33. Ground-floor plan and typical upper floor plan

FIG. 23. Wenzel Hablik. Exhibition Building, Project 1921. Perspective drawing

FIG. 24. Ludwig Mies van der Rohe and Philip Johnson, and Severud Associates. Seagram Building, New York, 1954–58. Elevation of steel frame and concrete walls

to the gods."[43] To be human is to be engaged in the making of art, to be both *homo faber* and *homo sapiens*, in practice. Thus, Barthes's understanding that "functional beauty does not reside in the perception of the good 'results' of a function, but in the spectacle of the function itself, seized in the moment before it is produced; to seize the functional beauty of a machine or an architecture, is in effect to suspend time, retard usage to contemplate a *fabrication*."[44]

The tall buildings of the 1950s and onward became an art medium encompassing all the sophistication of the 1920s and 1930s European avant-gardes. Le Corbusier's inventions, the *pilotis* and the *brise soleil*, and Mies van der Rohe's steel structure and glass skyscraper, among others, opened significant avenues of creative experimentation. Space, fabric, and structure can be interrelated in complex and suggestive ways. Their interaction can at times have metaphoric effects.[45] The figure of the metaphor—whether Charles Baudelaire's *correspondances*, Pound's and Fenollosa's ideogram, Eisenstein's montage, I. A. Richard's "interaction" or Barthes's "structure"— is a key critical tool.[46] Between the elements of a metaphor as well as its context a "resonance" can occur. This was the case with a few early tall buildings notably the Reliance, Guaranty, and Wainwright, and of course with the Statue of Liberty, but it is not until the postwar period that it is clearly implemented in new tall buildings.

The rhetoric of modern tall buildings is generative, and more so than their programmatic or urbanistic aspects. Tafuri and others have identified this clearly. Tall buildings are forms of persuasion constructed out of figures of a kind of speech, as well as material objects and building systems. In fact, those systems and materials serve as means to those figures, whether the figures are viewed as anarchic individuals or as ensembles. Robin Evans, for example, has shown how the mirror-finished cruciform columns of Mies van der Rohe's 1929 Barcelona Pavilion appear to "hold the roof down onto the walls, as if it were in danger of flying away. They hold it down more surely than they hold it up."[47] Just because a building structure looks rational does not mean it is. Critics often delight in exposing this contradiction, or labor to deny it. What is more useful is to see how the ambiguity itself constructs the meaning as metaphor.[48]

Mies van der Rohe's Crown Hall at the Illinois Institute of Technology in Chicago (1952–56) is a case in point. There is a skillful ambiguity between structural columns supporting the roof trusses and "nonstructural" mullions. In fact, the "mullions" on the side walls parallel to the trusses do support the roof. But more astonishing is the fact that, from the inside, it appears that the columns and mullions merge and all look alike, and the ceiling ap-

pears to float, independent of all of them. Eero Saarinen's General Motors Technical Center (1947–56) accomplishes a similar ambiguity by using the curtain-wall mullions as roof-supporting columns.[49] Gordon Bunshaft's and Paul Weidlinger's brilliant Beinecke Rare Book and Manuscript Library at Yale (1963) takes this even further, foreshadowing Herzog & de Meuron's manipulation of flat texture as material simulation. The Seagram Building, while technically not as advanced as these buildings, has even greater rhetorical power. Its siting, the deployment of dark and reflective surfaces and materials, the careful proportioning of the mass are all admirable. But it is Mies van der Rohe's transformation of the I-beam, gradually detaching it from its structural function, as he progressed from the Lake Shore Drive Apartments to the Seagram Building, to a sharp-edged synecdoche, that most clearly demonstrated the rhetorical effectiveness of abstracted structural geometries and elements. It is truly the reinvention of classicism put at the service of the projection of a corporate and urbane identity.

For Le Corbusier, "the 'orders' are replaced by *brise-soleils* which give scale and meaning to the facade through the representation of the hierarchy of spaces within the building."[50] But whereas sections of Le Corbusier's projects, for instance the Unité d'Habitation, Marseille (1946–52), show his plastic handling of structure, a section of the Seagram Building (Fig. 24) clearly shows the pragmatic and dissociated quality of the actual structure.[51]

Admitting the rhetorical to the architecture of tall buildings does not diminish its poetic capacities.[52] Indeed, it may be that the relationship of rhetoric and poetics is the dialectic most useful to any effort of interpretation. Rhetoric is the art of persuasion, and poetics the theory of making and judging poetry. They are inextricable. Northrop Frye sees rhetoric either as persuasion ("applied literature") or ornament ("the *lexis* or verbal texture of poetry").[53] Both are useful critical concepts. This dialectic goes back to the ancient Greeks and the most productive debates in Athens among the advocates and critics of democracy, most notably Socrates and Plato.[54] That rhetoric and poetry were illusory distractions from the true dialectics of philosophy was Plato's powerful antidemocratic argument. The interesting question of rhetoric and poetics, as it is applied to the interpretation of tall-building architecture, is then arguably a question about democracy. These "anarchic individuals" are, in a sense, diverse "speech acts" in the large agoras of our modern cities. They are not monuments, except perhaps on rare occasions when they come together as ensembles, such as Rockefeller Center. Like Auguste Rodin's *Burghers of Calais* (1884–86) and Alberto Giacometti's aptly named *City Square* (1948), they represent the demos.

THE POSTMODERN SKYSCRAPER

The architect-engineers Pier Luigi Nervi and R. Buckminster Fuller were invited to give the Charles Eliot Norton Lectures on Poetry at Harvard in 1961 and 1962, respectively. Both instances indicated a recognition of the poetic force of their work and its relevance to the culture. The architectural practices of both men integrated art and science. For a generation of architects and engineers, it seemed admirable that men like Nervi "combine two opposite frames of mind in one person: the synthetic, intuitive, artistic approach together with the analytic, mathematical, scientific approach."[55] The work of Nervi, and others like him, such as Félix Candela and Éduardo Torroja, was inspiring because it seemed to prove that beauty and truth could be one. This platonic fantasy seemed possible because the mathematics of thin concrete-shell design, the medium of choice, was both simple in formulation and endlessly rich in formal potential. It was like the idea of a generative grammar, which the linguist Noam Chomsky inaugurated in the mid-1950s.[56] Using a set of simple rules, he showed how the infinite richness and diversity of human creativity could emerge.

The idea of structural rationalism, at least in its postwar version, is closely related to this idea of grammar and simplicity. It is really no less than the aesthetics of structuralism itself. In structuralism, "what we generally call the signified—the meaning or conceptual content of an utterance—is now to be seen as a meaning-effect, as the objective mirage of signification generated and projected by the relationship of signifiers among themselves."[57] From the works of Nervi to the writings of Barthes, and from the "tensegrity structures" of Fuller to the fractal geometry of Benoît Mandelbrot, there is a common love of beauty as manifest in homologies of patterns, of structures, of natural forms and mathematical formulas, across scale and medium. The metallurgist and critic Cyril Stanley Smith ar-

gued that there is a "converse relationship between aesthetics and metallurgy,"[58] that it is the aesthetic drive that motivates the craftsman to invent new materials and techniques, which, in turn, lead to new technology and finally scientific discovery.[59]

One of the most influential architect-engineers of the postwar period, Myron Goldsmith of Skidmore, Owings & Merrill, apprenticed with both Nervi and Mies van der Rohe, and was also very much influenced by the writings of D'Arcy Thompson[60] on the similarity of natural forms at different scales, and the limits imposed on these similarities by gravity. Goldsmith taught a design studio with the structural engineer Fazlur Khan, also of Skidmore, Owings & Merrill, at the Illinois Institute of Technology for a number of years.[61] Together they experimented with structural forms for tall buildings, including varieties of braced cores, braced exteriors, rigid combinations of frames and braced cores, and ultimately the braced or rigid tube frames that became the structures of the very tall buildings built in the late 1960s and early 1970s. Their work was systematic, and relied on the use of numerical calculation on digital computers from early on. They were able to consider three-dimensional frames and hybrid structures, such as diagonally braced (or trussed) frames or shear walls linked to orthogonal, rigidly connected (or moment) frames (Fig. 25), and were also rigorous in their experimentation with both steel and reinforced concrete, alternating the application of their structural ideas between the two.[62] They were able to test their ideas on numerous commissions at Skidmore, Owings & Merrill and to learn from the work of other engineers and architects who had been inspired by their propositions.

The idea of the perimeter tube frame is a case in point. The first appearance of this was in the Chestnut-DeWitt Apartments (1961–65) by Myron Goldsmith, Bruce Graham, and Fazlur Khan of Skidmore, Owings & Merrill, followed shortly thereafter by their Brunswick Building (1962–66). This

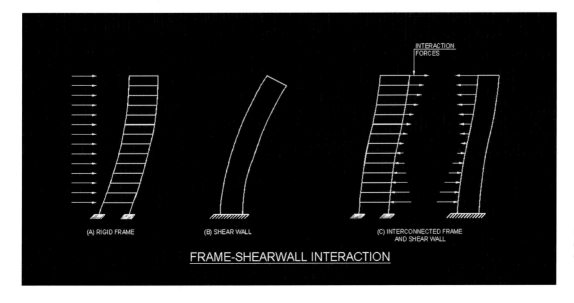

FIG. 25. Skidmore, Owings & Merrill. Diagram of interaction between frame and shear wall, c. 1960

form was adapted skillfully for the CBS Building in New York (1961–65) by Eero Saarinen. But where Skidmore, Owings & Merrill had made the tube out of a gridded frame, Saarinen and the engineers Paul Weidlinger and Mario Salvadori pushed the closely spaced columns beyond the floor beams, an approach adopted shortly thereafter by Minoru Yamasaki for the World Trade Center towers. Ironically, their emphasis on the columns of the tube frame was a return to the example of Adler's and Sullivan's Guaranty and Wainwright buildings, now reinterpreted to have all the verticals as primary structure. An aesthetic reinterpretation of the frame passed through a period of abstract and rhetorical development to re-emerge as the formal source of a new structural principle.

What Fredric Jameson characterized as the "relief of the postmodern"[63] has had both a productive and an alienating effect. Fuller declared in 1969 that all ideological dogmas would be "resolved" by the computer.[64] Certainly the computer, like the telescope, has opened a new universe of form and patterns, and served as a model for other forms of inquiry. It has also reinforced the kinship of science and art,[65] as the interest of science has moved to "systems of greater complexity, for methods of dealing with complicated nature as it exists."[66] The contemporary Pop and Fluxus productions illustrated wonderfully in Wolf Vostell's and Dick Higgins's *Fantastic Architecture*,[67] including Fuller's 1965 Tetra City (Fig. 26), constitutes only one of many manifestations of the energetic joining of multiple scales and practices of those movements.[68] At the same time, there is "the 'effacement of the traces of production' from the object itself, from the commodity thereby produced" that is characteristic of postmodern reification.[69] This tension between production and alienation is present in the development of tall buildings from the 1960s onward.

Pop Art and the related Archigram group, as well as the Situationist and Megastructuralist movements in architecture, worked through "play"

to achieve an influential body of work that is utopian, delirious, and even at times colossal.[70] The design and construction of the Centre Pompidou (1971–75) in Paris by the team of Renzo Piano and Richard Rogers was the first clear emergence of this line into the public realm.[71] While Louis I. Kahn's and Anne Tyng's 616-foot-tall Office Tower proposal for Philadelphia (Fig. 27) could be considered a precursor, given Piano's apprenticeship in that office, the Centre Pompidou clearly initiated the production-oriented practices that followed in Europe, both in its architects' work and in that of Norman Foster.

Foster's Hong Kong and Shanghai Bank in Hong Kong (1979–86) (Fig. 28) shares with the Centre Pompidou and Kahn's 1952–57 project, a lineage going back to Fuller's explorations in triangulated geometries and their techno-utopian association. But while Piano and Rogers, and the structural engineers Peter Rice and Edmund Happold, were looking for ways to show what Rice called the "trace of the hand,"[72] Foster and the engineer Jack Zunz (a colleague of Rice at Ove Arup & Partners) were re-forming their work to a machined anonymity.

Even so, both were able to achieve a result with strong popular appeal. Both the plaza in front of the Centre Pompidou and the public space in the Hong Kong and Shanghai Bank are modern piazzas.[73] And both their interiors have a level of detail and craftsmanship that, not unlike earlier Victorian works in Great Britain, afford a humanistic intimacy to which its occupants seem to respond well.

FIG. 26. R. Buckminster Fuller. Tetra City, San Francisco, Project, 1965. Photomontage

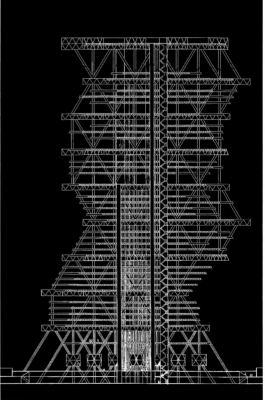

FIG. 27. Louis I. Kahn and Anne Tyng. Office Tower, Philadelphia, Project, 1952–57. Section

FIG. 28 Foster and Partners, and Ove Arup & Partners. Hong Kong and Shanghai Bank, Hong Kong, 1979–86. View of atrium

FIG. 29. Jørg Schlaich. Solar Chimney, Manzanares, Spain, 1980–81. The Solar Chimney produces energy by heating air under its expansive glass base; the heated air then rushes up through the chimney driving a turbine, thus producing power. This prototype operated as an effective alternative power source from 1983 to 1986.

Around the time the Centre Pompidou was being built, Happold and Arup collaborated on the Multihall at Mannheim (1970–75) with the architect Frei Otto. This biomorphic freeform timber dome required a convergence of computer-based calculations of complex geometries and structural behavior, and the use of physical models and testing that set the pattern of collaborative, empirical, and visibly "made to order" (even if highly computerized and machined) as opposed to mass-produced work.[74] Indeed, Frei Otto's one-time collaborator Jørg Schlaich's recent work in designing very tall solar chimneys in the 1980s (Fig. 29),[75] and the projects by the Arup engineers Peter Rice and Tom Barker, with Piano and then with Rogers, making early use of computational fluid dynamics to simulate large-scale air movements inside and around large buildings, are extensions of this focus on experimentation and production and the architectural use of their traces.

In the United States at that time, the completion of the Hancock and Sears towers in Chicago and the World Trade Center in New York represented, for the most part, the end of any integrated attention to production and experimentation. The World Trade Center towers were the work of structural engineers Leslie Robertson and John Skilling, whose intensity of thought on their structure has not been rivaled in the United States. Robertson standardized the geometry of the perimeter tube and the panelized floor structure in order to achieve large-scale prefabrication and rapid assembly. Recognizing the directional variation of wind loads, the so-called "wind rose,"[76] and the wind shadowing between the towers, he also used, for each floor, beams and columns made of plates all the same thickness but of varying strength properties as a way to accommodate the asymmetrical load-and-stress patterns—an ephemeral rather than formal expression. This was mass customization on a giant scale, and a level of complex project management comparable to the contemporaneous Apollo 11 lunar expedition. The concentration of invention and integration across disciplines as well as the unexpected minimalist sculptural presence of the towers had been rivaled in New York only by the Statue of Liberty.

In Chicago the Sears Tower by Bruce Graham and Fazlur Khan of Skidmore, Owings & Merrill has a comparable sculptural power (reminiscent in stance of Rodin's *Balzac*) and specific relationship to the wind environment.[77] Its asymmetrical form as well, like that of the World Trade Center towers, gives it a strong role as a means of orientation in the city and a dynamic quality. While New York's twin towers were each independent single-framed tubes, the Sears Tower is itself a bundle of nine such tubes tied together. Both are constructed forms whose innovative structures are legible to the knowledgeable but still somewhat ambiguous behind either the shear black facade of the Sears Tower or the reflective ribs of the Trade Center.

The Hancock tower in Chicago, on the other hand, appears emphatically structural; the large-scale, three-dimensional trussed tube is even a mega-structure (Fig. 30). The detailed computer analysis by Fazlur Khan and his team revealed that the large diagonal members, ostensibly there as

FIG. 30. Bruce Graham and Fazlur Khan, Skidmore Owings & Merrill. John Hancock Building, Chicago, 1970, under construction

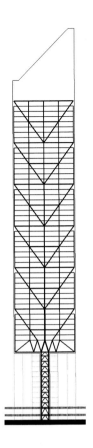

FIG. 31. Hugh Stubbins and William LeMessurier. Citicorp Center, New York, 1974–77. Elevation of structural frame

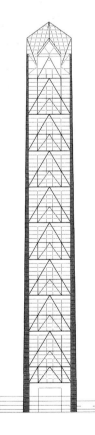

FIG. 32. Helmut Jahn and William LeMessurier. Bank of the Southwest, Houston, Project 1982. Elevation of structural frame

wind bracing, drew a large portion of the building's gravity load, owing to the relative rigidity of the large diagonals and smaller columns, and the unavoidable triangulation of gravity columns, beams, and diagonal wind braces. What appears to be a clear diagram is in fact a hybrid. This discovery actually led to the most inventive tall-building structures of the late 1970s and 1980s, notably Citicorp Center (1974–77) by Hugh Stubbins and William J. LeMessurier, the Bank of the Southwest project in Houston (1982) by Helmut Jahn and LeMessurier (Figs. 31, 32), and the Bank of China (1982–89) by I. M. Pei and Leslie Robertson (Fig. 33). The structural strategy for these buildings was to combine a small number (four to eight) of columns with cross bracing connecting them through the building; this combined the functions of carrying gravity load and effecting wind resistance into one integrated system.[78] In the case of LeMessurier's structures, the system consists of interlocking planar trusses. In the Bank of China, Robertson and Pei extended the idea into a three-dimensional triangulated space frame (Fig. 34).

In all three cases, however, the innovative structure is only partially expressed. Unlike the Hancock tower with its exoskeleton, these buildings have manifestly thin curtain walls tightly wrapped around their forms. This is especially true of Citicorp and the Bank of China where the triangulated structure is entirely, or selectively, suppressed and displaced[79]—a practice fully in the tradition of Mies van der Rohe's Seagram Building. The Bank of China further succeeds in appearing to be a rare crystal object on a refined pedestal, appealing both to Chinese connoisseurship and early modern expressionist precedents.

This surface flatness characterizes some of the best tall-building designs of that period in the United States. The Hancock Tower in Boston (1977) and Fountain Place in Dallas (1986) by

Henry Cobb of Pei Cobb Freed & Partners have a minimalist sculptural purity and minimalist structure (the latter by the skilled protégé of Fazlur Khan, the structural engineer Prabodh Banavalkar) that achieve a kind of "almost nothing" and flatness, skillfully expressing the developers' quest for a maximum "net-to-gross" floor area ratio.

THE CONTEMPORARY TALL BUILDING AS METAPHOR

When John [Cage] *and I first thought of separating the dance and the music, it was very difficult, because people had this idea about the music supporting the dance rhythmically. I can remember so clearly—in one piece I made some kind of very big movement, and there was no sound at all, but right after it came this incredible sound on the prepared piano, and I understood that these two separate things could make something that couldn't have happened any other way.*
—Merce Cunningham, 2002[80]

In the early twentieth century, the creative step in American tall-building design, from the Chicago School to Frank Lloyd Wright, was to turn to the plan as the generator of form. A similar key turn in contemporary tall-building design has been toward the whole building section. This was signaled by Rem Koolhaas's book *Delirious New York* (1978), which drew attention to the surrealist section of the Downtown Athletic Club, New York (1926) by Starrett & Van Vleck. At the same time, both Skidmore, Owings & Merrill and Norman Foster were experimenting with the organization of office floors in clusters grouped around common spaces, usually atria, and accessible by express elevators stopping only once per cluster, with escalators in between. Skidmore, Owings & Merrill's experiment was short-lived, but for Foster this became a key

FIG. 33. I. M. Pei, Pei Cobb Freed & Partners, and Leslie Robertson. Bank of China, Hong Kong, 1982–89, under construction

FIG. 34. I. M. Pei, Pei Cobb Freed & Partners, and Leslie Robertson. Bank of China, Hong Kong, 1982–89. Construction photograph showing a corner of the three-dimensional triangulated space frame before the corner concrete columns were poured

FIG. 35. Foster and Partners, and Ove Arup & Partners. Commerzbank Headquarters, Frankfurt, 1991–97. View in downtown Frankfurt

concept that he developed through to the present with increasing sophistication. The earliest example was the low-rise Willis Faber Building (1971–75) in Ipswich, itself an extraordinary concentration of inventive form, materials (the earliest use of planar-bolted glass walls), and social organization. The later Hong Kong and Shanghai Bank extended both the use of modular office "villages" for organization and the intensity of technical and material invention. In Foster's Commerzbank in Frankfurt (Fig. 35), Swiss Reinsurance Headquarters for London (pages 72–79), and his office's World Trade Center proposal (pages 164–169), as well as Rem Koolhaas's Togok (XL Towers) for Seoul, Korea (pages 144–149), and Central Chinese Television (CCTV) Tower for Beijing (pages 102–109), the range of experimentation, and accomplishment, is impressive. With the exception of Foster's World Trade Center proposal, which was developed with the New York structural engineers Ysrael Seinuk and Ahmad Rahimian, these projects were all designed in collaboration with the structural engineers at Ove Arup & Partners, notably Rem Koolhaas's collaborator Cecil Balmond. These tall buildings are, or would be, landmarks. In the case of Koolhaas's Togok (XL Towers), this is projected by grouping buildings into integrated ensembles, in the tradition of Rockefeller Center. The Togok project, while alluding to the vertical patterns of Rockefeller Center and more so even to its successors (Time-Life, McGraw Hill, etc.) by Harrison and Abramowitz along Sixth Avenue, literally adds a new dimension by leaning two of its six slender towers into and alongside three of the others to form large-scale A-frames. An equally large-scale "collar" truss ties these frames to the other towers, and forms a high-altitude datum. The resulting structural assembly is then interconnected with resilient dampers to control wind-induced vibrations. The CCTV project is formally less complex than the Togok project. Sculpturally, it

is close to some of Isamu Noguchi's work (Fig. 36) and that of Tony Smith.[81] The structure is developed on the facade as a triangulated grid of varying density reflecting the stress distribution. The internal program is segregated into zones that differentiate the space in the sections.

Norman Foster's tall-building projects are equally ambitious, although less Dionysian than Koolhaas's. The Frankfurt Commerzbank was a breakthrough as the first demonstrably "ecological" skyscraper, with natural light and views, and organized in modules or "villages" of interior space. The building also marked a calmer formal stratagem, closer in spirit to Mies van der Rohe's minimalism than the earlier Hong Kong and Shanghai Bank project, while still demonstrating an unusually progressive social agenda in the organization of spaces. With this and the later Swiss Reinsurance Headquarters and World Trade Center projects, Foster also developed a more legible and less rhetorical structure than that of the Hong Kong building.[82] The "diagrid" of expressed diagonals and suppressed horizontals in both projects still maintains some of the ambivalence of expression of the Miesian tradition. After all, the diamond pattern is only part of the triangulated structure. In both the Swiss Reinsurance Headquarters and World Trade Center projects, these white lines serve effectively as highlights, sharpening the optical clarity of the distinct forms. The horizontal floor beam elements, while part of the truss structure, are visually suppressed.

At the same time, formal exuberance has clearly emerged in force in the design of contemporary tall buildings. Philip Johnson with his AT&T Headquarters (1984)[83] and Gordon Bunshaft, with his last and most minimalist skyscraper (1983) in Jedda, had already introduced the effect of what Barthes called the "miniaturization of the tower," a kind of mingling of model and souvenir (*maquette et bibelot*)—something not only to hold and, in a

FIG. 36. Isamu Noguchi. *Energy Void*, 1971

sense, domesticate but also to receive the projection of one's own potential power as maker. It may be that the remarkable popular support that met Foster's scheme for the World Trade Center site had not only to do with his re-creation of the twin towers and the project's sculptural, structural, and ecological qualities, but also with this scalability.

The Swiss Reinsurance Headquarters at 30 St. Mary Axe has a different, if equally ambitious, urban charge. Despite its size—at 590 feet (180 meters), only sixty percent of the height of the Eiffel Tower—it will become a distinct focus, or landmark, for London. The building form, in effect that of a bullet, is circular in plan and tapers both at the top and, slightly, at its base. The shape reduces the apparent size of the building seen close-up, and seems to have also reduced the degree to which the wind is deflected by the building down to the street level. There are spiraling atria that divide the floor plates into distinct work areas and that link these visually across floors. The atria can also draw natural ventilation as they bridge areas of positive and negative wind pressure. The exterior structure is a rigid and redundant system that can efficiently resist the wind load and effectively redistribute the gravity load in case an accidental blast damages any element (the building was constructed on the site of a damaging IRA attack). One striking, if invisible, detail is the adjustment (or truing) of the building frame and the way it was accomplished during construction. A number of pockets left open in the slab allowed radial adjustment of the exterior frame to the floor, like the spokes on a bicycle wheel.

The tall building as a landmark, such as Swiss Reinsurance, can re-orient an older city center, mark new areas of development, or create the image of new cities. Teodoro González de Léon's Arcos Bosques Corporativo buildings in Mexico City (pages 62–67) have had this effect for its new area of high-technology development. It also belongs to a group of new buildings, starting with Peter Eisenman's proposed Max Reinhardt Haus for Berlin (pages 42–45) and Koolhaas's CCTV Tower, that form a closed, looped shape. This has impor-

tant advantages for circulation, for safety (offering many more routes of escape in a fire), and for structure. It also offers a much larger area of accessible space at the highest level. Since September 11, this has become a consistent element of many proposals for tall buildings.

There is clearly an increased complexity in the development of tall buildings, which is visible in their sections. They no longer comprise the simple extensions of repeated commercially viable floor areas. For one thing, there are the social and environmental agendas of architects like Norman Foster. But also there is the imperative of mass-transportation access, the notion of the tall building as transit hub, pioneered with the World Trade Center.[84] This strengthens the ecological justification of tall buildings as energy and open-space savers (and advances the late-capitalist objective of routing workers through shopping malls). Thus we have generated multiple hybrid programs consisting of transit, shopping (often all the way to the upper floors), entertainment, and observation. Hans Hollein's Monte Laa PORR Towers is a clear manifestation of this (pages 38–41), as are of course the United Architects and Norman Foster proposals for the World Trade Center site (pages 156–163, 164–169). It also recalls Hollein's iconic Aircraft Carrier City of 1964 (Fig. 37)—an ironic but also telling precursor to this use of program to make unexpected form.

This also links to the increasing sculptural ambition of many recent projects. In one sense, this is a return to the traditions of *colossi*, of the Statue of Liberty and its precursors. One project of this type is the proposal for the New York Times Headquarters on Manhattan's West Side (pages 80–85) by Frank O. Gehry, with David Childs of Skidmore, Owings & Merrill, a highly accomplished abstract colossal sculpture. The facade is made of "wrappers"[85] of curved sheets of vertically ribbed glass curtain wall and extends far above the roof level as a huge parapet. These wrappers are held away and distinct from the building structure. The floor plates vary according to the billowing profile of the exterior. The structure itself, a simple frame, is of the usu-

FIG. 37. Hans Hollein. Aircraft Carrier City in Landscape. Project, 1964. Perspective, cut-and-pasted printed paper on gelatin silver photographs, mounted on board

ally deadpan straight-man kind favored by Gehry.

Kohn Pedersen Fox's Kowloon Station Tower (pages 150–155), shares with Gehry's project the effect of a glass facade peeling from its mass. The tower is one of two very tall developments over new mass-transit stations in Hong Kong. The other tower, by César Pelli, is across the water on Hong Kong Island. Each is over 1,542 feet (470 meters) high, taller than the Sears Tower. The Kowloon tower is located on an unusually deep and narrow deposit of very soft soil, so that its orientation bridging this underground valley at an angle to the local city grid, in fact, literally marks the contours of the land it is founded on. As with most of the new very tall buildings (over 1,300 feet, or about 400 meters), the structure is made up of a continuous concrete-wall-enclosed core and a series of outrigger steel trusses at regular vertical intervals that are tied to eight very large columns on the perimeter aligned with the faces of the core shaft. In Asia, these outrigger trusses, occupying full-story height, can easily occur at the "refuge" floors that are required for fire safety at about 200-foot intervals. This "mast" concept is the same as Eiffel's pylon and outrigger truss structure for the Statue of Liberty. The great benefit is to free the facade from the structural role it had in the perimeter-tube frames of the Sears and World Trade Center towers, opening the view, and opening the possibility of sculptural play.

The idea of a "mast" tied with outriggers to perimeter columns (or "stays") was explored by Fazlur Khan in the 1960s but did not emerge in the design of tall structures until the 1980s proposal for the Miglin-Beitler tower in Chicago by César Pelli and the engineer Charles Thornton, and the same team's Petronas Towers in Kuala Lumpur (1991–97). The re-emergence of this structural type is due in part to the increasing attention to wind-induced vibrations that cause discomfort for workers in very tall buildings. Since mass and damping are generally more effective at reducing vibrations than stiffness, the trend, starting in the 1980s, was to increase building density and add mechanical damping to tall slender structures.[86]

The Jin Mao Tower in Shanghai (pages 138–143) and the 7 South Dearborn mixed-use tower project for Chicago (pages 170–175), both by the Skidmore, Owings & Merrill office in Chicago, have adopted this core-mast idea. On the Jin Mao structure this allows the building facade considerable freedom, while providing a strong underlying formal structure to the plan; a kind of Greek-cross configuration is maintained owing to the geometry of the core, outriggers, and exterior stay-columns. What is most interesting about Jin Mao, however, is the sectional inversion that takes place at the top floors where the program shifts to a hotel. Here, in the tradition of John Portman's atrium hotels, the shaft of the core is made void as the elevators and serv-ices are shifted to one side. The core concrete walls remain, turning into the separation between the room and the continuous balcony facing into the huge atrium. This topological inversion is both simple and quite awe inspiring, and has become a tourist attraction in its own right.

The 7 South Dearborn project was to be 2,000 feet tall and include three digital transmission antennae. Indeed, the tower is not easily categorized since its raison d'être was to have been the revenue from the antennae. The program starts with offices at the base, apartments in the middle, and broadcast studios at the top. The separation into these modules is articulated with gaps made possible by the fact that the floors of the top three modules are cantilevered from the central concrete core. There is only one set of outriggers on this mast, located at the top of the base portion. The fact that the area of the core near the top is greater than the residential area around it creates an ambiguity of type. It also tends to a very direct expression of functional equilibrium and formal simplicity.

The idea of having gaps belongs to a rather unusual long-term experiment on the part of Skidmore, Owings & Merrill in collaboration with Nicholas Isyumov of the Boundary Layer Wind Tunnel in Canada. Isyumov and Baker, as well as Baker's predecessors at the firm, have investigated ways to reduce the effective wind load on tall structures by "confusing" it, as Baker describes it. It turns out that one of the principal sources of problematic vibrations in tall slender structures is the aerodynamic phenomenon of vortex shedding (Fig. 38). This effect occurs when a steady wind, at a particular velocity (not necessarily that great) interacts with a building's size and shape such that regular vortices form alternately at opposite corners of the leeward side. These vortices form and detach steadily at regular intervals. When that temporal rhythm coincides with one of the building's natural

Fig. 38. Peter Voke, with Nathan Steggel. Diagram of vortex shedding (produced via computational fluid mechanics)

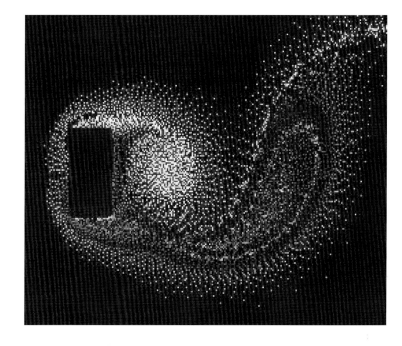

periods of vibration, the sway that results (actually perpendicular to the wind's direction) can be felt. To counteract this, Isyumov and the Skidmore, Owings & Merrill engineers have experimented with large holes in buildings and, in this case, gaps to disrupt the vortex formations. On 7 South Dearborn it worked well enough in the wind tunnel to reduce the wind effects by twenty-five percent.

Another way to counter wind vibration is to use dampers. These can be large masses located high in the building (such as the Citicorp Center) on sliding surfaces and between carefully calibrated springs. These are designed to move opposite to the building motion and dampen its effect. Or, they can be mechanical dampers, like shock absorbers (such as the viscoelastic dampers on the World Trade Center), that directly absorb energy.

The Highcliff and Summit apartment buildings in Hong Kong by Dennis Lau Wing-kwong and the engineer Ad Gouwerok of Magnusson Klemencic Associates (pages 110–115), make use of a very effective damping device, the tuned "sloshing" damper. This is made up of two sets of paired water tanks that allow water to slosh back and forth between the tanks, both countering the building sway and dissipating energy through the water's turbulence. The apartments themselves, especially in Highcliff, have a nautical quality, narrowing as they do from the center core and ending in the master bedroom and bathtub at the "prow." These apartments have extraordinary views since the building is not only 827 feet (252 meters) tall but is perched high on the hillside overlooking the harbor. Some apartments are at least 1,300 feet (400 meters) above sea level. The pairing of the two towers, one convex the other concave, and their extreme slenderness, shapes the space around them as well. The towers are, in fact, quite prominent in the skyline of Hong Kong Island, as they extend above the top line of the mountains, so their identity is as a pair, not twins, and their spatial interplay is as interesting as their individual qualities.

The use of damping devices to reduce wind vibration and the design of tall-building ensembles are both literally the means of making a design out of interactions. The Togok (XL Towers) by Rem Koolhaas is an excellent example of both. The design uses the differential movements of the towers to drive dampers and dissipate wind energy: the prevention of physical resonance, as it were, juxtaposed with the metaphoric resonance between things. The JR Ueno Railway Station Redevelopment tower project by Arata Isozaki, with the engineer Toshihiko Kimura and his associates, uses extremely large trussed struts to help stiffen the narrow direction of the building against earthquakes (pages 116–121). The tower is part of a projected complex of retail and office spaces on top of a train station, a program that was applied with very interesting results in Japan in the 1980s

(at Kyoto and Nagoya). The struts are attached to the distinct structural "belt trusses" at the fifth points of the tower height.[87] The projected cladding geometry is also quite distinct, creating both lenticular cuts at the corners and a pillowing effect between the "belts."

Renzo Piano's projected London Bridge Tower, at 1,016 feet (310 meters) and seventy-seven-stories tall, is a slender pyramid clad in what Piano describes as "shards" of glass (pages 122–125). The building site is directly above London Bridge Station and includes offices, live/work, public, residential, and broadcast facilities, in that order, from bottom to top. The structure is also a stayed mast consisting of a concrete core (to be cast using a self-supporting "jump" form—one where the form is in parts that move by each one "jumping" over the one just above, rather than "slipping" as a whole, as is sometimes the method) and steel floor framing, outriggers, and composite steel and concrete stays, or "outrigger" columns. The central heating system uses the waste heat from the office areas to heat the residential areas. The mechanical engineer John Berry of Ove Arup & Partners predicts that, overall, the carbon dioxide emission will be about 9,000 tons a year or about two-thirds that of a typical office building. There is interaction in the actual heat exchange, just as there is interaction of structural movement and dampers to dissipate the dynamic energy of the wind. Increasingly, buildings are active participants, even to actual motion, fluid flows, and exchanges of energy with the environment. It is no wonder that the mapping of these exchanges and physical patterns has become a source of structural ornamentation as rich and organic as Louis Sullivan's and Dankmar Adler's earlier dialogues on ornament and pragmatism.

The structural engineer Cecil Balmond of Ove Arup & Partners has explored this pattern-making, drawing on number theory[88] and Mandelbrot's theories of fractal geometry to create some remarkable structural patterns, notably in the Victoria and Albert Museum with Daniel Libeskind, and currently on the CCTV exterior bracing structure with Rem Koolhaas. Starting from a uniform grid, Balmond and his team evolved a pattern reflecting the varied stresses in the diagonal members of the CCTV facade by reducing their number where stresses are low.

A similar strategy was used on the Edificio Manantiales, Santiago, Chile, by Luis Izquierdo W., Antonia Lehman S. B., Raimundo Lira V., José Domingo Peñafiel E., and the engineer Luis Soler P. (pages 34–37). Here, responding to the need to resist earthquake effects, the designers devised a combined system of a concrete core and partial perimeter bracing. The perimeter bracing is made of eleven-and-one-half-inch (29.6 cm) diameter round concrete struts, both vertical and inclined, that counter-intuitively increase in extent with the height. The reason is that they serve to counteract the building's tendency to twist (torsion) caused by the placement of the concrete core off center (necessary to preserve good leasable space). As the building plan grows out at the lower floor, that eccentricity diminishes and the necessity for the exterior bracing is lessened.

For both the CCTV and Edificio Manantiales structures, the configuration required repeated iteration of the analysis to arrive at a balanced result. Each step in that interaction was then the evaluation of the interaction of structural parts, an adjustment (or tuning), and a replay. The final design is the trace of that development and, in effect, the evidence of a physical process. Louis Sullivan would have appreciated this fine balance of rhetoric and poetry.

THE STANDARD MODEL

The so-called Standard Model of subatomic particle physics, first formulated in the 1970s[89] and largely confirmed by experiments since, accounts for the basic effects of three of the four fundamental forces: electromagnetism, the strong and weak forces, and gravity. The model diagrams the interactions of matter particles (the fermions: electrons, quarks, muons, and taus) and force carriers (photons, gluons, and other bosons). The model allows for their particular interactions, which have so far given a good prediction of the complex interactions observed in high-energy particle physics experiments. This is no orbital model of stars and planets. Its geometry is far more complex, akin to the universes of Paul Klee and John Cage, and it exceeds physical intuition. So, perhaps the present postmodern culture might at last elude the hold of idealism in Western thought and come to accept poetry and rhetoric as closer to the real, not, as Plato argued, the faint shadow of a reality available only to an elite few.

The best recent evidence of this may have been the recovery efforts at the World Trade Center site following the disaster and horror of September 11. It was the best evidence, since the 1960s, of democracy's effectiveness at the ground level. People worked and argued to solve problems and keep everyone safe. Things got taken care of through individual initiative tempered with deliberation, a flexible re-ordering of priorities, and a supple executive structure.

Democracy is itself a "standard model," and the best tall buildings are, at times, its best advocates on the skyline. They can inspire society by the dignity of their language, the example of their social and environmental thoughtfulness, and the evident quality of the social processes by which they are made. The trace of the hand, as Peter Rice would say, is the "speech act" of the worker, there to please and inspire his fellow citizens.

Since the completion of the World Trade Center towers in 1973, there has been a redirection of energy within the United States practice of tall-building design toward an industrial method, much like its automobile industry: the body is styled but the chassis is standard. This worked quite well for American developers but led, in general, to silent buildings.

It is encouraging that some architects, such as Norman Foster and Frank Gehry, have drawn their technologies and some inspiration from aerospace. Prototyping and computer-aided customized manufacturing processes have helped them make not only complex buildings but rich and complex practices within their own offices—constructive in both the social and artistic realms.

Once again, more balanced teams are coming together to collaborate on projects, recapturing some of the quality of engineering design that existed in the 1950s and 1960s, which was mostly lost with the advent of post-1969 formalism.[90] Here, the evolving model, drawing from the example of filmmaking, seems to help provide a framework: an audience that has learned to appreciate the difference in art between the actor's work and the director's work, and the pleasure that is found in discovering and distinguishing those differences, can begin to see the gain achieved in strong collaborations. The work of Frank Gehry and Rem Koolhaas has grown stronger in collaboration with more thoughtful and creative engineers, such as Jørg Schlaich and Cecil Balmond.

Ove Arup once described his theory of the architectural "star system" as the right choice of a metaphor or idea toward which to navigate a project, regardless of the occasional detours. This can be a metaphor that unites the energies of a team, much like the historic convergences that form the vortices of Ezra Pound's *Cantos*. After all, the history and practice of tall-building design shows that, like the history of jazz, it is utterly urban, street smart, and at its best in those rare moments when everyone is playing well together.

Notes

1. Henry James, "New York Revisited," *Harper's Monthly Magazine* 112 (February 1906): 402; quoted in Sarah B. Landau and Carl Condit, *Rise of the New York Skyscraper, 1865–1913* (New Haven: Yale University Press, 1996): 285.

2. For a list of Osama bin Laden's prospective targets, see Eric Lichtblau, "Bin Laden Chose 9/11 Targets, Al Queda Leader Says," *The New York Times* (March 20, 2003): A22.

3. Marvin Trachtenberg, *The Statue of Liberty* (New York: Viking Press; London: Penguin Books, 1976): 35.

4. Ibid.: 79.

5. Charles Talansier, "La Statue de la Liberté éclairant le monde," in *Le Génie Civil* (Paris, 1883): 15; quoted in Henri Loyrette, *Gustave Eiffel* (New York: Rizzoli, 1985): 100.

6. For an excellent discussion of expressionist architecture and its universalist politics, see Alan Colquhoun, *Modern Architecture* (Oxford and New York: Oxford University Press, 2002): 89.

7. Françoise Fromonot, *Jørn Utzon: The Sydney Opera House* (Corte Madera, Calif.: Ginko; Milan: Electa, 1998): 91, 107.

8. Sergei M. Eisenstein, "Synchronization of Senses," in Jay Leyda, ed., *The Film Sense* (New York: Harcourt, Brace, 1942): 69.

9. Ibid.: 74–75.

10. Ernest Fenollosa, *The Chinese Written Character as a Medium for Poetry*, ed. Ezra Pound (San Francisco: City Lights Books, 1968). See also, Sergei M. Eisenstein, "The Cinematographic Principle and the Ideogram," in idem, *Film Forum* (New York: Harcourt, Brace, 1949): 28–44.

11. Fenollosa, *Chinese Written Character*: 26. See also Hugh Kenner, *The Pound Era* (Berkeley and Los Angeles: University of California Press, 1971).

12. Ezra Pound, *Gaudier Brzeska: A Memoir* (New York: New Directions, 1970): 92.

13. Alan Colquhoun, "The Displacement of Concepts in Le Corbusier," in idem, *Essays in Architectural Criticism* (Cambridge, Mass.: MIT Press, 1981): 52.

14. The Reliance Building is always photographed from the southeast at three-quarter view because it has only two sides of white terra cotta. The other two are plain brick party walls. See Joanna Merwood, "The Mechanization of Cladding: The Reliance Building and Narratives of Modern Architecture," *Grey Room* 04 (Summer 2001): 53–69. With its 1999 restoration, the Reliance Building has gone from the drab gray of early engravings and black-and-white photographs to a brilliant white. This radiance is a reminder of the key role of color and glaze in lightening the appearance of curtain walls and giving even the truly massive masonry Monadnock Block dazzling highlights.

15. Colin Rowe, "Chicago Frame," in idem, *The Mathematics of the Ideal Villa and Other Essays* (Cambridge, Mass.: MIT Press, 1976): 89–117. In full: "An autonomous structure perforates a freely abstracted space."

16. Prior to the December 6, 1968, editiion of the New York City Building Laws, the code did not require any wind-force calculations for buildings under one-hundred feet, nor under 150 feet before 1935 (James Colgate and Mark Topping, Department of Buildings, and Irwin Cantor, personal communications to the author, 2003).

17. Adrian Stokes, "Venice," in Lawrence Gowing, ed., *The Critical Writings of Adrian Stokes: Volume II, 1937–1938* (London: Thames & Hudson, 1978): 91.

18. Ibid.: 93.

19. James, "New York Revisited": 402.

20. See Louis H. Sullivan, *Kindergarten Chats (Revised 1918) and Other Writings*. Documents of Modern Art (New York: Wittenborn, Schultz, 1947).

21. William Le Baron Jenney, "The Chicago Construction, or Tall Buildings on a Compressible Soil," *Inland Architect and News Record* 18 (November 1891): 41; quoted in Merwood, "Mechanization of Cladding": 56.

22. Manfredo Tafuri, "The Disenchanted Mountain: The Skyscraper and the City," in Giorgio Ciucci, Francesco Dal Co, Mario Manieri-Elia, and Manfredo Tafuri, *The American City: From the Civil War to the New Deal* (London: Granada, 1980): 390–391.

23. Ibid.: 419.

24. Ibid.: 448. The 1982 film *Blade Runner* offered a contemporary analogue to Tafuri's interpretation in its intensely architectural and urban character. The movie set, part collage, image, and representation, conveyed the potential emotive impact of a city—the very impact that both Eliel Saarinen and Hugh Ferris hoped to create with architecture.

25 Walt Whitman, "I Sing the Body Electric," in idem, *Leaves of Grass*. Inclusive Edition, ed. Emory Holloway (Garden City, New York: Doubleday, 1926): 79–80.

26. See Carol Willis, ed., *Building the Empire State* (New York: W. W. Norton, 1998): It is striking how similar the Empire State Building is to Eliel Saarinen's Grand Hotel scheme (1923), especially in early renderings that do not include the antennae.

27. Ibid.: 11. The Chrysler Building required 21,000 tons for 850,000 square feet, or about fifty pounds per square foot as well.

28. The structural engineers Weiskopf & Pickworth did the same on the Daily News Building by Raymond Hood, using braced frames in one direction (the narrow one) and relying on the interaction of frame and masonry infill in the other for wind resistance. In the case of the Daily News, the architect also allowed the outer wythe of ceramic glazed white brick to run continuously and be self-supporting rather than run as a "curtain" relieved on each floor. Again, the pragmatism of New York designers tended to mix methods without much conceptual consistency.

29. Le Corbusier, *When the Cathedrals Were White* (Cornwall, N.Y.: Reynal & Hitchcock, 1947): 54–56.

30. Tafuri, "Disenchanted Mountain": 483–484.

31. The Monadnock Block by John Wellborn Root is a sixteen-story-tall office building of load-bearing exterior brick walls that are up to six feet thick at the base. It represented the limit of bearing-wall construction at the birth of steel-skeleton framing. Despite this, the simplicity of its lines, the deep glow of purple indigo and slightly glazed brick, and the clear expression of mass is a forerunner of later rationalist structural expression.

32. John Wellborn Root, "A Great American Problem," *Inland Architect and New Record* 15, no. 5 (June 1890): 69. I wish to thank Henry Cobb for giving me a copy of this essay.

33. Ibid.: 70.

34. Colquhoun, *Modern Architecture*: 237.

35. Rowe, "Chicago Frame": 99.

36. The 2001 restoration of the Lever House replaced the two-piece spandrel glass panel with a single piece covered by an applied horizontal metal girt. The original two-piece spandrel glass panels had on occasion been replaced since 1952 by glass of a darker blue than the original, weaving a random pattern of subtle color differences. See color illustration in Colquhoun, *Modern Architecture*: 238 (fig. 163).

37. The orthogonal crystal forms of Bruno Taut's glass architecture, of Kazimir Malevich's *Arkitektens* (c. 1924), and of Eliel Saarinen's 1920s skyscraper designs, had a strong influence on Hugh Ferris's and Raymond Hood's skyscraper massing experiments.

38. Root, "Great American Problem": 69.

39. Ibid.: 70.

40. Montgomery Schuyler, "Some Recent Skyscrapers," *Architectural Record* 22, no. 3 (September 1907): 164.

41. Roland Barthes and André Martin, *La Tour Eiffel* (Paris: Delpire, 1964): 33. Trans. Guy Nordenson. "*C'est qu'ici les raisons utilitaires, si ennoblies qu'elles soient par le mythe de la Science, ne sont rien en comparaison de la grande fonction imaginaire qui, elle, sert aux hommes à être proprement humains. Cependant, comme toujours, le sens gratuit de l'oeuvre n'est jamais avoué directement: il est rationalisé sous l'usage.*"

42. Ibid.: 64. Trans. Guy Nordenson. "*L'architecture est toujours rêve et fonction, expression d'une utopie et instrument d'un confort.*"

43. David Jones, "Art and Democracy" in *Epoch and Artist* (New York: Chilmark Press, 1959): 87–89.

44. Barthes and Martin, *Tour Eiffel*: 64. Trans. Guy Nordenson. "*La beauté fonctionnelle ne réside pas dans la perception des bons 'résultats' d'une fonction, mais dans le spectacle de la fonction elle même, saisie dans un moment antérieur à ce qu'elle produit; saisir la beauté fonctionnelle d'une machine ou d'une architecture, c'est en somme suspendre le temps, retarder l'usage pour contempler une fabrication.*"

45. For an excellent discussion of metaphor, rhetoric, and poetics, see Alex Preminger, ed., *Princeton Encyclopedia of Poetry and Poetics* (Princeton, N.J.: Princeton University Press, 1965): 490, 702.

46. See Alison Smithson, ed., Team 10 Primer (Cambridge, Mass: MIT Press, 1968) for the application of ideograms and for I. A. Richard's ideas on architecture and planning.

47. Robin Evans, "Mies van der Rohe's Paradoxical Symmetries" in idem, *Translations from Drawing to Building and Other Essays* (Cambridge Mass.: MIT Press, 1997): 242.

48. See William Empson, *Seven Types of Ambiguity* (New York: New Directions, 1966): 2. "Metaphor is the synthesis of several units of observation into one commanding image; it is the expression of a complex idea, not by analysis, nor by direct statement, but by a sudden perception of an objective relation." Also note Empson's deconstruction of the idea of "atmosphere" as a psychological, and not poetic, effect.

49. Reinhold Martin, *The Organizational Complex: Architecture, Media, and Corporate Space* (Cambridge, Mass.: MIT Press, 2003): 242.

50. Colquhoun, *Modern Architecture*: 211.

51. T. S. Eliot's critical concept of the "dissociation of sensibility" is applicable. Writing of the metaphysical poets, he observed that "the structure of the sentences ... is something far from simple, but this is not a vice; it is a fidelity to thought and feeling," and that "the poet must become more and more comprehensive, more allusive, more indirect, in order to force, to dislocate if necessary, language into his meaning," in idem, *Selected Essays* (New York: Harcourt, Brace, 1964): 245, 248.

52. The Girasole apartment building in Rome (1949–50) by Luigi Moretti is an astonishing example of the rhetoric and poetic deployment of space and structure with profound results.

53. Marrin T. Herrick, "Rhetoric and Feeling," in Preminger, *Princeton Encyclopedia*: 704.

54. Josiah Ober, *Political Dissent in Democratic Athens* (Princeton, N.J.: Princeton University Press, 1998).

55. Pier Luigi Nervi, *Structures*, trans. Giuseppina and Mario Salvadori

(New York: F. W. Dodge, 1956): vi.

56. See Noam Chomsky, *Syntactic Structures* (The Hague: Mouton, 1957) and idem, *Aspects of the Theory of Syntax* (Cambridge, Mass.: MIT Press, 1965): 3–10.

57. Fredric Jameson, *Postmodernism, or, The Cultural Logic of Late Capitalism* (Durham: Duke University Press, 1991): 26.

58. Cyril Stanley Smith, "Structure, Substructure, Superstructure," in Gyorgy Kepes, ed., *Structure in Art and in Science* (New York: George Braziller, 1965): 29.

59. See Cyril Stanley Smith, *A Search for Structure* (Cambridge, Mass.: MIT Press, 1981), and idem, *From Art to Science: Seventy-Two Objects Illustrating the Nature of Discovery* (Cambridge, Mass.: MIT Press, 1980).

60. D'Arcy Thompson, *On Growth and Form* (Cambridge and New York: Cambridge University Press, 1961).

61. Myron Goldsmith, *Myron Goldsmith: Buildings and Concepts* (New York: Rizzoli, 1987).

62. Goldsmith was the Spinoza of Skidmore, Owings & Merrill structural rationalism, carefully developing the formal implications of purist structural ideas. His 50 x 50 House drawings for Mies van der Rohe's office of April 8, 1952, already show his synthetic genius; see Phyllis Lambert, ed., *Mies in America* (New York: Abrams, 2001): 459. From the Brunswick Building to the Rochester Building, the Sears Tower, and the Haj Terminal at Jedda airport, his influence on Fazlur Khan and others at Skidmore, Owings & Merrill is pervasive.

63. Jameson, *Postmodernism*: 313.

64. R. Buckminster Fuller, *Operating Manual for Spaceship Earth* (New York, Pocket Books, 1970): 120.

65. There was an MIT vortex in the 1960s: from Noam Chomsky's linguistics to Warren McCulloch and Jerome Y. Lettvin's physiological studies of the brain (see Warren S. McCulloch, *Embodiments of Mind* (Cambridge, Mass.: MIT Press, 1965); from Cyril Smith's studies of the metallurgical arts and sciences to Giorgio di Santillana's writings on the astronomical discoveries of the pre-Socratics; and from Norbert Wiener's cybernetics to the "discovery" of chaos science by Edward Lorenz. This was a powerful, if still unrecognized, renaissance in American intellectual life.

66. Smith, "Structure, Substructure, Superstructure": 41.

67. "This documentation … is architecture!" From Wolf Vostell and Dick Higgins, *Fantastic Architecture* (New York: Something Else Press, 1969). Trans. of the German ed.: *Pop Architektur, Concept Art* (Düsseldorf: Droste, 1969).

68. Billy Klüver, Julie Martin, and Barbara Rose, eds., *Pavilion, by Experiments in Art and Technology* (New York: E. P. Dutton, 1972); this is the account of a collaborative experiment for a fog-enveloped polygonal structure for multimedia performances at Expo '70 in Osaka Japan.

69. Jameson, *Postmodernism*: 314.

70. Colquhoun, *Modern Architecture*: 226. Also see, Jacques Derrida, "La structure, le signe et le jeu dans les discours des sciences humaines," in *L'écriture et la différence* (Paris: Editions du Seuil, 1967): 409–428. Noam Chomsky told the author in 1977 that Derrida had written to him before coming to the United States the first time to ask if he would be safe there.

71. See Colquhoun, "Plateau Beaubourg" in idem, *Essays in Architectural Criticism*.

72. Peter Rice was referring, in particular, to the evidence of the casting and assembly of structure being easily legible. See his *An Engineer Imagines* (London: Artemis, 1994).

73. The open space under the Hong Kong and Shanghai Bank is used on weekends as a meeting place and "job fair" for mostly Filipino housekeepers. It seems that in some tropical cities such open spaces under buildings are well-used public places (another example is Lina Bo Bardi's Museo de Arte São Paulo, Brazil).

74. The Mannheim Multihall is notable both as a free form (akin to Heinz Isler's contemporary investigations into freeform thin concrete shells), and as the vortex that brought Frei Otto, Ove Arup, and Edmund Happold together. Since the dome was a compressive inversion of Otto's tensile investigations, he needed help from Arup and Happold to understand the limits imposed by buckling on its thinness. The project introduced Happold and, through him, Peter Rice to lightweight structures and to the problem of analyzing large displacements in geometrically nonlinear structures. While Rice and Happold (who later left Arup to start his own office) evolved the "dynamic relaxation" approach to handling these analyses, Jørg Schlaich, a past collaborator with Otto on the Munich Stadium in 1972, took a separate analytical tack using the finite-element methods. Happold, Rice, and Schlaich later developed rich and diverse bodies of work based on both these analytical and detailing practices. The Multihall is a Tempio Malatestiano of postwar structural design; see Institute for Lightweight Structures, *IL-13 Multihalle Mannheim* (Stuttgart: Heinrich Fink, 1978).

75. Alan Holgate, *The Art of Structural Engineering: The Work of Jørg Schlaich and His Team* (Stuttgart, Edition Axel Menges, 1997): 273–275.

76. The wind rose is a diagram of the maximum velocities of the wind measured for a particular period of time and plotted over the cardinal directions. It shows the directions of prevailing winds for a particular location.

77. The wind-tunnel studies for the Sears Tower by Alan G. Davenport and his colleagues demonstrated that the orientation of the top twenty stories of the building was critical to the overal aerodynamics of the structure. The top part of the building consists of two of the nine ninety-foot-square plan modules. Because these were oriented with the long axis perpendicular to the prevailing westerly winds, the effects of vortex shedding were minimized and, in fact, created a damping effect on the building. (Herbert Rothman and John Zils, personal communications to the author, 2003).

78. See Darl Rastorfer, "William J. LeMessurier's Super-tall Structures: A Search for the Ideal," *Architectural Record* 173, no. 1 (January 1985): 141–151.

79. The Bank of China takes the form of a crystal on a carved wood stand, a typical collector's *objet d'art* in China. The base of the tower, a postmodern study in geometric decoration, clearly reinforces this reading, which would have appealed to the gentlemen bankers that were Pei's clients. The crystal form lent itself to the space structure design that Robertson and Pei devised for it, but the purity of the geometry ruled throughout, forcing the structural geometry back from the concentric surface lines of the curtain wall. The corner mega-columns of concrete cleanly resolve that structural "eccentricity" so that it benefits the structure and its construction. The facade lines, in turn, rewrite the traces and widths of the structural geometry for a deceptively pure reading. These poetics and rhetoric of the building's structure and appearance are worthy of the Seagram Building.

80. Merce Cunningham, quoted in Calvin Tomkins, "The Creative Life: A Troupe Turns Fifty," *The New Yorker* (July 8, 2002): 26.

81. There is also an interesting link between the work of Rem Koolhaas and Alberto Giacometti. Koolhaas's brilliant competition entry for the Bibliothèque National in Paris is quite similar to Giacometti's *Cage* sculptures in terms of the use of a box of things (quite like a box of toys) suspended in space. This gives both works a frame and therefore an intense negative space between the positive volumes, a fact Giacometti and Koolhaas each develop elsewhere.

82. The trusses that support the floors below on the facade of the Hong Kong and Shanghai Bank are the same as the interior trusses that do the same with the omission of the top horizontal "chord" member. This omission reinforces the appearance of suspension but elides the fact that the trusses also play a key role as the beams of the "mega" moment frames that resist winds in the east–west, or longitudinal, direction of the building.

83. The structure of the AT&T Building was Robertson's last tall-building structural design in the United States. It is another brilliant example of Robertson's use of steel. The structure is part truss, part steel shear walls (an innovation at the time), and all clear and symmetrical. Its craft is a suitable match to the care with which the thick stone curtain wall is detailed, and its disappearance behind that wall is appropriately postmodern.

84. The idea of a tall building astride a train station has a sad history in Manhattan, with the demolition of Penn Station and the construction of the Pan Am Building over Grand Central Station (despite the romance of its helicopter pad). It has become, however, an important type around the world.

85. See Fredric Jameson's discussion of the "strategy of the wrapper" in idem, *Postmodernism*: 97–129; also see his analysis of Gehry's Santa Monica House.

86. The Canadian wind engineer Peter Irwin transformed the design of tall thin Manhattan towers in the 1980s (the three towers around Carnegie Hall and the Millenium Hotel across from the World Trade Center site, all by the structural engineer Jacob Grossman) by emphasizing the importance of density as a means of limiting wind vibration. Since steel buildings are less than half the density of concrete ones (twelve vs. twenty-five pounds per cubic foot) and since inexpensive foundations on rock are the norm in Manhattan, the very slender (up to 1:15) towers of that era were all made of concrete.

87. One of the fascinating and unwritten aspects of modern tall-building design is the frequent use of proportional relations, often related to the golden section and the Fibonacci series (1:2, 2:3, 3:5, etc.), to regulate geometries.

88. See Cecil Balmond, *Number 9* (Munich: Prestel, 1998) and idem, *Informal* (Munich: Prestel, 2002). The idea of expressing the geometries of nonlinear or chaos processes and patterns has appeared more frequently in the 1990s, on such buildings as the Edificio Mantiales, Steven Holl's Simmons Hall at MIT, and Balmond's and Koolhaas's CCTV Tower.

89. See Steven Weinberg, *The Discovery of Subatomic Particles* (New York: Scientific American Library, 1983); and Gordon Kane, "The Dawn of Physics Beyond the Standard Model," *Scientific American* 288, no. 6 (June 2003): 68–75.

90. See discussion of 1969 Conference of Architects for the Study of the Environment (CASE) held at The Museum of Modern Art, in Arthur Drexler, *Five Architects* (New York: Oxford University Press, 1975).

Projects

Note to the Plates: The twenty-five buildings presented in this section are organized by height, in a progression from the shortest to the tallest. All were designed during the last decade; some of them are built, others are in construction, and still others remain projects that will not be constructed.

Wherever possible, building dates include both the design and construction processes. The heights of the buildings, given in feet and meters within the project headings and also as an index on the right-hand pages, are measured from the ground to the roof or, where applicable, to the tops of antennae.

Principal architects and engineers are listed above the descriptive texts for each work; the full credits and technical specifications for the buildings are given in the Appendix at the back of the book. Photographic credits can also be found at the end of this volume.

Edificio Manantiales

Santiago, Chile
1997–99

Architects: Luis Izquierdo W., Antonia Lehmann S. B., Raimundo Lira V., José Domingo Peñafiel E.
Engineer: Luis Soler P.

187 FEET (57 METERS) HIGH

Four architects and a structural engineer collaborated on the Edificio Manantiales, an office building that is remarkable for its consistent inventiveness and strong urban advocacy. The project is of modest height, only 187 feet tall, and is located in an area of Santiago that has been transformed in the last decade from a low-density residential neighborhood to a rapidly growing but mostly unplanned commercial district of seven- to twenty-story buildings.

The building is divided into two sectors: one is a seventeen-story-high tower, and the other is a ten-story-high building. The taller of the two has floor plates of 2,600 square feet, and the shorter one has floor plates of 7,298 square feet. All of this surmounts five levels of underground parking. The geometry of the building is coordinated with the parking layout so that no structural transfers are needed. The parking area is arranged in half levels with connecting ramps, and uses an innovative system of large portholes with fans to circulate fresh air down and around each level.

The site is on the southeast corner of two streets that form an angle slightly sharper than the standard ninety degrees, but the building is orthogonal in plan and far enough from the street to avoid any setback regulations of the local zoning code. A projecting, suspended wall along the exit stair at the north side of the building marks the limit of the zoning envelope and the edge of the tower volume. Another wall, along the stair in the center of the east wall, closes the northeast edge of the seventeen-story tower and folds up and over the top of the roof deck.

The east and south facades, which intersect at the corner, are set with open strips of butt-glazed windows between exposed concrete one meter (three feet, three inches) deep and upturned edge beams. The core is located in the center of the base of the building and the parking below, and emerges on the north facade of the tower with the open pair of exposed concrete scissor stairs. Besides these exit stairs, the core includes four

elevators enclosed in concrete shear walls. These provide much of the lateral resistance to the wind and to the potentially damaging earthquake ground motion possible in Chile. On the lower ten floors, frames of closely spaced wide concrete columns and beams, a kind of punched wall, in fact, add to that resistance (and also form screens to limit views to and from the adjacent buildings). However, at the west and north setbacks to the upper floors these frames are cut off. Thus, the core becomes eccentric to the floor plate.

To compensate for this and for the potentially damaging motion due to torsion that would occur in an earthquake, the designers created a completely original variable bracing scheme that, counter-intuitively, increases in density with height. The members of this diagonal bracing system are circular concrete sections cast in place using PVC pipe of an inside diameter of eleven and five-eighths inches (all but two are this size). Their number was decided by an interactive process of computer analysis aimed at achieving the closest balance to the eccentric core's effect. This order is most evident on the east facade where its pattern is a direct measure of the effects of torsion. The longer south facade structure is more complex, as it registers these effects at the top as well as the effect of the stiff moment frame at the lower levels to balance the east frame. The resolution of the bracing at the base creates a colonnade along the entrance, marked at the start by the only two different circular members, thirteen inches in interior diameter. These slightly larger members are a direct response to the overturning forces concentrated at the southeast corner of the frame above.

This project represents a close collaborative effort by a large team of designers. Every detail, from the well-formed exposed concrete structure to the controlled disposition and geometry of each element, material, and system, communicates a strong desire for order and civility.

—Guy Nordenson

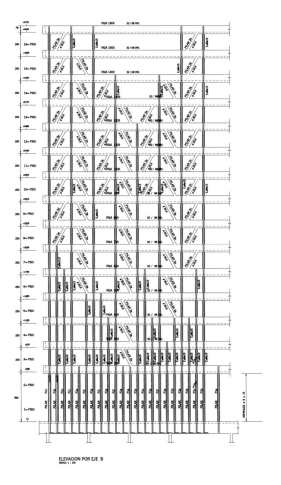

ELEVACION POR EJE B

ABOVE Structural elevation, south facade
OPPOSITE View of southeast corner

187 ft. (57 m)

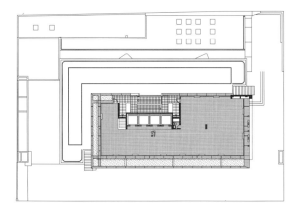

Plan, floor 17

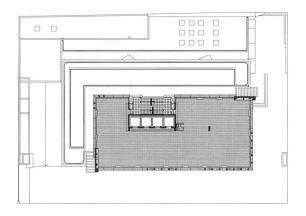

Typical plan, floors 12–15

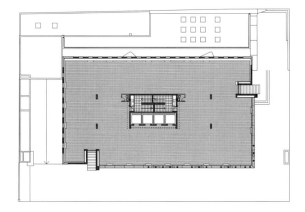

Typical plan, floors 4–10

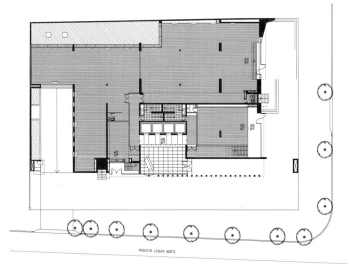

Site plan and ground-floor plan

Close-up view of southeast corner

Elevation, east facade

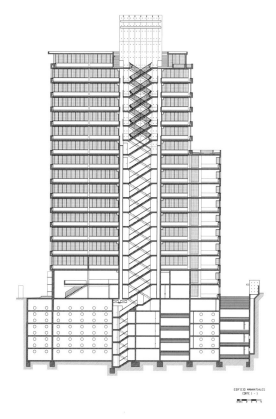

View of northeast corner

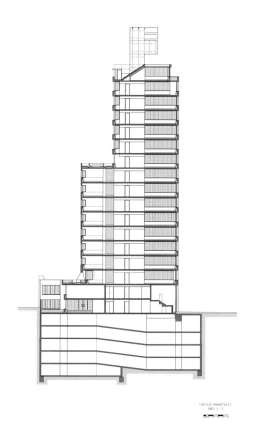

Transverse section, north–south

Longitudinal section, east–west

187 ft. (57 m)

Monte Laa PORR Towers
Monte Laa Development

Vienna, Austria
Design, 2000—02; projected completion, 2006

Architect: Hans Hollein | Atelier Hollein
Engineer: Joseph Janda | Projektierungsbüro für Industrie-,
  Hoch- und Tiefbau

361 FEET (110 METERS) HIGH

Hans Hollein's PORR Towers for Vienna are part of a master plan for the Monte Laa Development. The development incorporates offices, housing, and parks on the former PORR storage yard, in an attempt to extend Vienna's urban fabric and revitalize a fragmented area of town east of its medieval core. The site is the highest in the city, and divided by an expressway constructed in the 1970s that provides one of two entries into the city from the south. Hollein's design, which spans the highway, comprises two slim, glass-clad towers capped with 100-foot-high cantilevers, elevating the level of urban activity to the sky.

The towers, linked at ground level by a central double-height lobby, each provide twenty-five stories of rentable office space and form the bases for the main architectural element at their highest levels—a horizontal network of conference rooms, press rooms, restaurants, auditoriums, and terraces spread over four levels of well-differentiated spaces. These rooms are connected at two upper levels by steel-framed bridges, which let out onto various rooftop terraces and gardens. Hollein has called the construction a "multifunctional agglomeration of flexible spaces" that provides "an ideal setting for meetings and conferences in areas of space and light."

The 460-seat auditorium as well as the meeting and press rooms above the north tower, for example, can all be turned into a large exhibition zone through the use of flexible partitioning. In the south tower, the lofty rooms function as direct extensions of the lobby below: express elevators connect a conference entry on the ground floor with the rooms above, a conference area, a 170-seat auditorium, and a restaurant. While modest in scale relative to other tall buildings, the towers create a conspicuous presence on the skyline, with their high sky-lobby cantilevers extending over their footprints and with one of these "arms" flashing a video billboard toward the expressway, flaunting their presence. Visible from the center of Vienna as well as the expressway, the towers are even more noticeable at night when they become illuminated and transparent.

Although its planned completion date is 2006, the project is a continuation of much of Hollein's thinking since the 1960s, when he first conceived, in masterful collages, towers in such iconic forms as aircraft carriers, telescopes, or spark plugs that formed images of an irresistible presence in an otherwise barren landscape. Hollein's twentieth-century agents of urbanism have now become twenty-first-century architecture in the Vienna Towers. Their upper floors also recall El Lissitzky's gravity-defying Constructivist compositions, even as they appear momentarily tethered.

—Tina di Carlo

View of south facade from expressway
(computer-generated image)

Perspective sketch showing south facade

361 ft. (110 m)

Aerial view from the north
(computer-generated image)

Model showing top-floor structures at night

View of west facades
(computer-generated image)

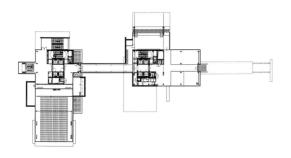

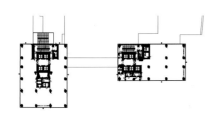

Study model

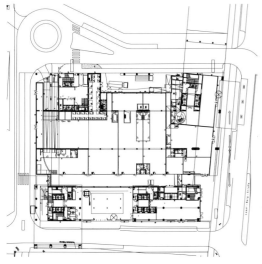

TOP TO BOTTOM
Plan of conference center, floor 26
Typical floor plan
Site plan and ground-floor plan

Transverse section, east–west

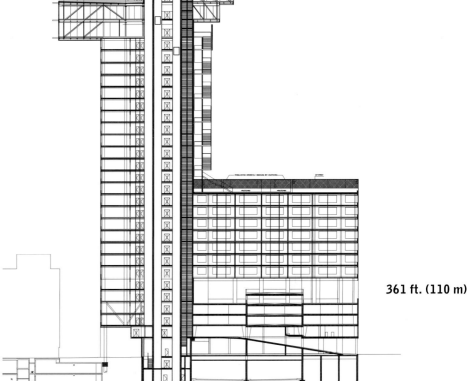

361 ft. (110 m)

Max Reinhardt Haus

Berlin, Germany
Project, 1992—93

Architect: Peter Eisenman | Eisenman Architects
Engineer: Severud Associates

420 FEET (128 METERS) HIGH

The project for Max Reinhardt Haus is a proposal for a reunified Berlin that was conceived by the architect Peter Eisenman shortly after the removal of the Berlin Wall in 1991. Its site is on the north bank of the Spree River, at the intersection of two of Berlin's most prominent and historically rich thoroughfares—the famous Unter den Linden and Friedrichstrasse. Beginning in 1919, the site was occupied by the Grosses Schauspielhaus, a fantastic Expressionist playhouse designed by Hans Poelzig for Max Reinhardt, a prominent theater producer in Germany, known for his energy and vision. Directly across the Spree River is a triangular site in front of the main railroad station for which Ludwig Mies van der Rohe designed his influential project for the first glass skyscraper in 1921.

In order to capture Reinhardt's legendary energy in a building named for him, Eisenman devised a prismatic form that creates a world unto itself and yet opens out to, and reflects, the constantly changing and multifaceted character of the city itself. Its one million square feet include office space, hotel accommodations, film and media auditoriums, retail space, a fitness center, offices for press and public relations agencies, a restaurant, and video and audio technology—in the architect's words, "a true heterotopia."

The building rises thirty-four stories above the ground, creating a folding arch of intersecting and overlapping forms that towers above Berlin's typical four-story landscape. Vertically folding on its core, it presents a unified structure that separates, compresses, transforms, and then rejoins itself horizontally at the roof level. The form was generated from three iterative operations performed on a Möbius strip, a three-dimensional geometric form with a single unending surface. The strip allows two dimensions to be folded into a single surface by twisting in on itself. In so doing it denies the traditional dialectic of inside and outside and, when appropriated to architecture, blurs the distinction between public and private.

In the first iteration, planes are generated from the extension of vectors and the triangulation of the surfaces; this triangulation permits the development of both a surface order for cladding and a trussed structure for vertical and lateral support. The second iteration inverts the strip, performs a similar operation to that of the first step, and then imprints these surfaces on the initial form, thereby creating a phantom or ghost. The third step maps an element of Berlin's history onto the form itself by folding large public space between the grid and floor plates of an already folded structure—a reference to the cubic volumes of the German neoclassical architect Karl Friedrich Schinkel. These voids seem to occupy the layered spaces of the floors as aggregates in a matrix and without any apparent effect on their makeup. According to Eisenman, this "suggests the presence of invisible and inaudible communications which, upon reception, shall become the stuff of daily life in the future." The building, whose height, crenellated form, and ghostly blue pallor create an imposing, ominous presence, looks forward to its own history and yet is imbued with energy and abstract formal references to past events, reflecting a continually shifting urban paradigm.
—Tina di Carlo

BELOW Sections
OPPOSITE Model

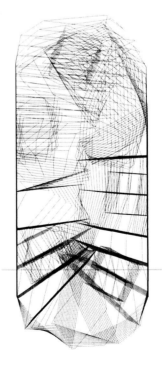

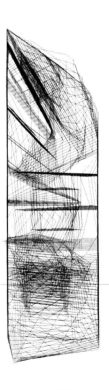

Section

Section

420 ft. (128 m)

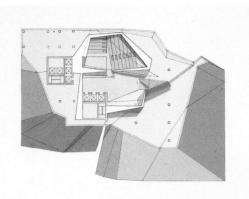

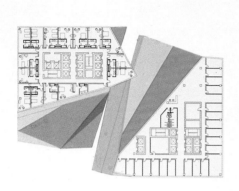

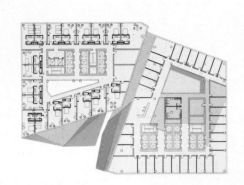

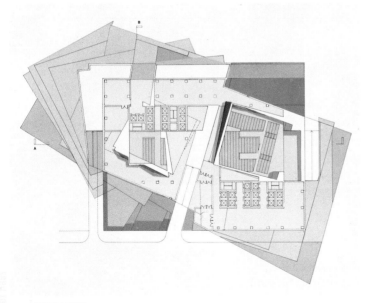

TOP TO BOTTOM
Plan, floor 29
Plan, floor 13
Plan, floor 3
Ground-floor plan

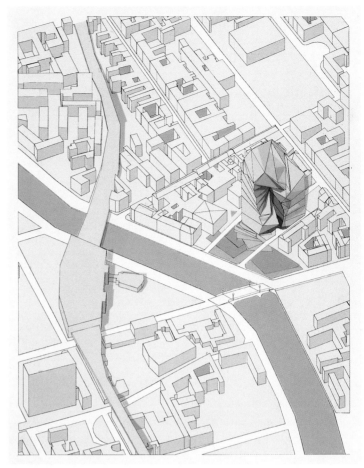

Axonometric view from the north
(computer-generated image)

Transverse section

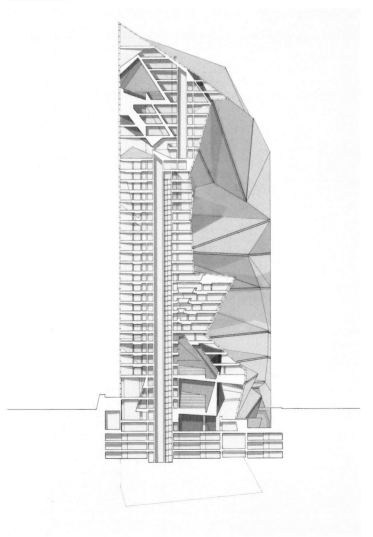

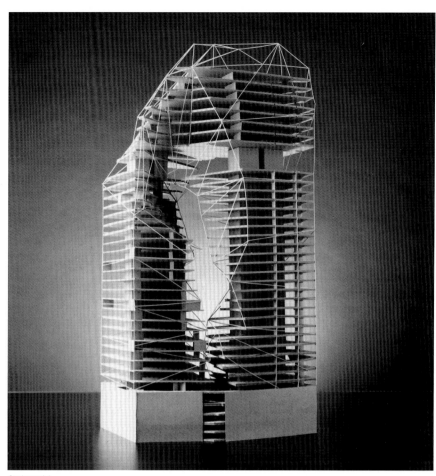

Study model

Longitudinal section

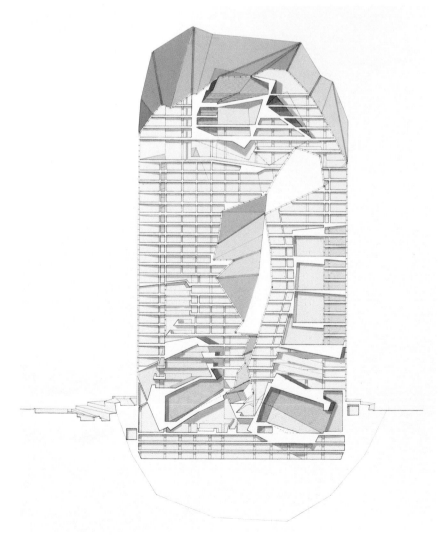

420 ft. (128 m)

Elephant and Castle Eco Towers

London, England
Project, 2000

Architect: Ken Yeang | T. R. Hamzah & Yeang
Engineer: Christopher McCarthy | Battle McCarthy

TOWER 1: 459 FEET (140 METERS) HIGH
TOWER 2: 240 FEET (73 METERS) HIGH

The Malaysian architect Ken Yeang's Elephant and Castle Eco Towers are part of an extensive 180-acre plan to redevelop south-central London. The complex is intended to offer over one million square feet of commercial space for shopping, 5,000 residences, offices, hotels, community facilities, and three major parks. Yeang's design—two tall sustainable residential structures totaling approximately 300,000 square feet of which twenty percent is dedicated to circulation and vegetation—reflects his contention that "the skyscraper offers the greatest possibilities for the recycling of precious resources."

The towers are intended to function together as a vertical city, or "a microcosm of the city itself," offering amenities found within a typical urban block: apartments, bars, restaurants, sports facilities, playgrounds, and parks. The central feature of each tower is a vertical landscaped environment, configured as two blocks sandwiching a weather-protected, landscaped core. Large intermittent voids progress from public parks and semiprivate entrance courts to private balconies, providing communal "sky pods" and "sky courts." The towers are situated to the east of a railway interchange that divides the overall site, and maintain a southern orientation that maximizes solar-heat gain during the winter and solar shading during the summer months. Large openings on the north and south facades provide ventilation and cooling, as well as cross-ventilation for the apartments. Operable shutters, adjustable according to season, further refine the air supply. In addition to creating a "greener" more humane environment, the landscaped spaces buffer wind as well as absorb and reflect a high percentage of solar radiation, thereby reducing ambient temperatures in the warmer months. Vegetation also serves to rehabilitate the site's ecosystem. The primarily passive low-energy system will be supplemented with a traditional electro-mechanical system to be used as needed.

The generative principle behind Yeang's bioclimatic design is that energy-efficient systems can transform architecture into a confident science, involving economy of means, efficient land use, and effective low-energy consumption. Yeang's tall buildings express a commercial commodity inextricably linked to its geographical context and immediate environmental conditions.

Residences range in size from studios and two-room apartments to penthouses, and can accommodate people of various ages and socio-economic backgrounds. Each unit has an entrance lobby, light wells, balconies, and shared secondary and tertiary open spaces, which re-create conditions at ground level "in the sky."

—Tina di Carlo

BELOW Section, preliminary scheme
OPPOSITE Model, Tower 1, from above

459 ft. (140 m)

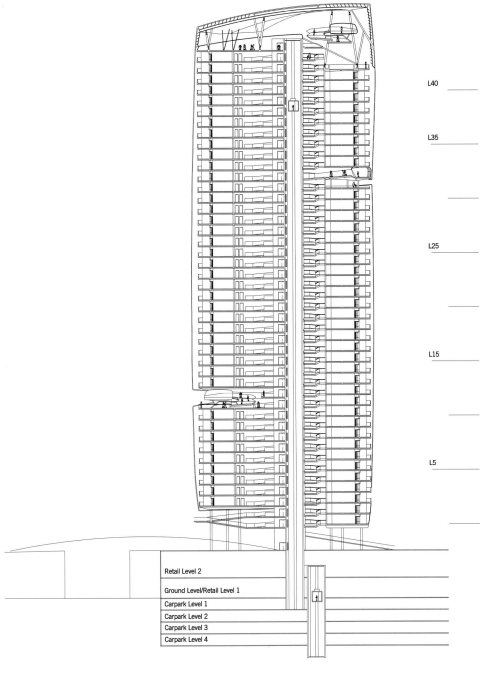

L40

L35

L25

L15

L5

| Retail Level 2 |
| Ground Level/Retail Level 1 |
| Carpark Level 1 |
| Carpark Level 2 |
| Carpark Level 3 |
| Carpark Level 4 |

Section, Tower 1

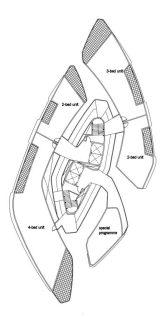

3-bed unit

2-bed unit

1-bed unit

4-bed unit

3-bed unit

3-bed unit

2-bed unit

2-bed unit

4-bed unit

special programmes

Typical floor plans

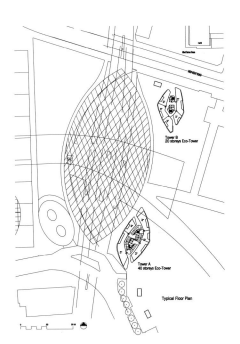

Tower B
20 storeys Eco-Tower

Tower A
40 storeys Eco-Tower

Typical Floor Plan

Site plan

Model, Tower 1, front and side elevations

Wind, sun, and climatization diagrams

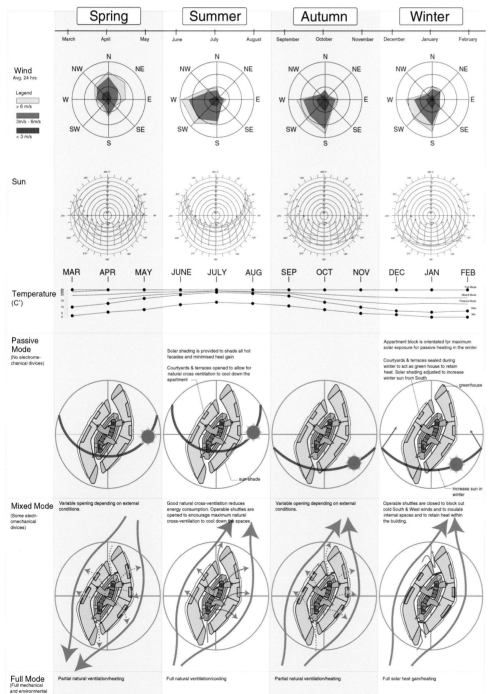

	Spring	Summer	Autumn	Winter
	March April May	June July August	September October November	December January February

Wind
Avg. 24 hrs

Legend
> 6 m/s
3m/s - 6m/s
< 3 m/s

Sun

MAR   APR   MAY   JUNE   JULY   AUG   SEP   OCT   NOV   DEC   JAN   FEB

Temperature (C°)
Full Mode
Mixed Mode
Passive Mode
Max
Min

Passive Mode
(No electrome-chanical divices)

Solar shading is provided to shade all hot facades and minimised heat gain.

Courtyards & terraces opened to allow for natural cross ventilation to cool down the apartment

Appartment block is orientated fpr maximum solar exposure for passive heating in the winter

Courtyards & terraces sealed during winter to act as green house to retain heat. Solar shading adjusted to increase winter sun from South

greenhouse

sun shade

increase sun in winter

Mixed Mode
(Some electromechanical divices)

Variable opening depending on external conditions.

Good natural cross-ventilation reduces energy consumption. Operable shuttles are opened to encourage maximum natural cross-ventilation to cool down the spaces.

Variable opening depending on external conditions.

Operable shuttles are closed to block out cold South & West winds and to insulate internal spaces and to retain heat within the building.

Full Mode
(Full mechanical and environmental systems)

Partial natural ventilation/heating   Full natural ventilation/cooling   Partial natural ventilation/heating   Full solar heat gain/heating

459 ft. (140 m)

Electricité de France (EDF) Headquarters

La Défense, Paris, France
1995–2002

Architect: Henry N. Cobb | Pei Cobb Freed & Partners
Engineer: Jean Heuber | SETEC

486 FEET (148 METERS) HIGH

La Défense is a business area on the outskirts of Paris where tall structures are permitted. Henry N. Cobb's Electricité de France (EDF) Headquarters building, located on an exceptionally prominent site there, overlooks the district's central open space. For Cobb: "The privilege of building here carries with it a corollary obligation to enrich the public realm of La Défense."

Driven by the geometry of its surroundings, the building's form and situation defer to its specific urban context. The placement of the building responds directly to the 1982–90 Grande Arche de la Défense by Johann Otto von Spreckelsen, which is a 348-foot-high hollowed-out cube conceived by the French president François Mitterrand as a twentieth-century Arc de Triomphe. The Grande Arche is placed directly on axis with the Arc de Triomphe to the southeast, but in plan the Arche's cube is skewed slightly, by seven degrees, shifting its facade slightly off this axis.

Cobb's EDF building is located along the axial route from the Arche to the Arc, which sets up the orthogonal framework for La Défense. From the center of the EDF building's circular canopy there is a direct site line to the center of the Grande Arche's monumental facade. The elliptical shape of the EDF tower specifically honors the Grande Arche by adopting its slightly canted orientation instead of being placed at ninety degrees to the axis, as are the other buildings in the area. This places the two buildings on parallel axes. The EDF tower, one might say, offers the Arche a geometric gesture of respect.

A defining feature of Cobb's building is the half-cone cutaway from the edge of the ellipsis above the entrance canopy. The top of the cutaway corresponds to the inner height of the Arche, and the shape of the semicircular void is an acknowledgement of the nineteenth-century monument, *La Défense de Paris*, which stands on a circular base directly in front of the building, as if the statue had emerged from the void. The statue, once the centerpiece of a roundabout when the area was a Parisian suburb, commemorates the defense of Paris during the Franco-Prussian War of 1870–71.

To accommodate the formal plasticity of the building, the structure is of reinforced concrete with a central slip-formed concrete core and perimeter columns supporting a flat-plate concrete slab. The circular stainless-steel-and-glass-clad canopy, seventy-two feet in diameter, is cantilevered over the entrance; its remarkable thinness is achieved by the use of welded-steel structural box girders. It appears to have sliced away the concave corner of the building, and creates an inviting gathering place: a location for arranged meetings, a shelter from the rain, and a spot from which to view the plaza and the monumental Arche de la Défense. Clearly concerned with humanizing the tower and improving community access, Cobb has created an inviting public space at the entrance to this private building.

—Bevin Cline

BELOW Perspective of northeast facade, by Paul Stevenson Oles
OPPOSITE View of northeast facade from plaza

486 ft. (148 m)

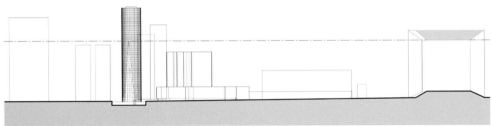

Site plan and elevation, showing the Grande
Arche de la Défense to the northwest of the tower,
their axial alignments, and alignment with the
inner height of the Arche

Site plan

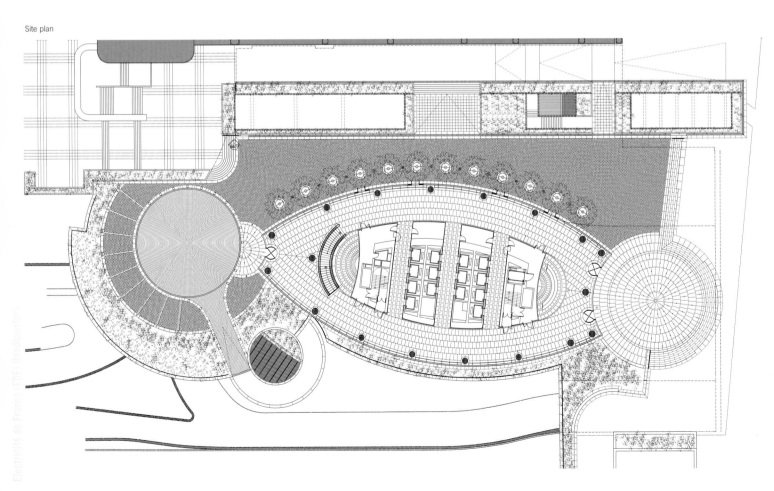

Close-up view of north facade, with nineteenth-
century statue *La Défense de Paris*

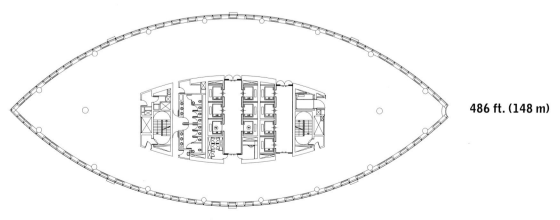

486 ft. (148 m)

Typical floor plan

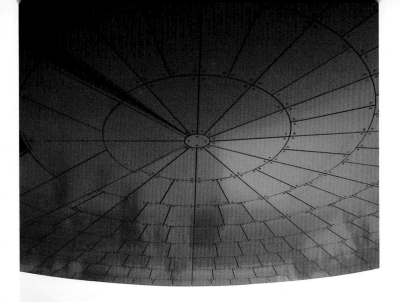

View from underneath canopy looking northwest
toward the Grande Arche de la Défense

Facade detail, half-cone cutaway

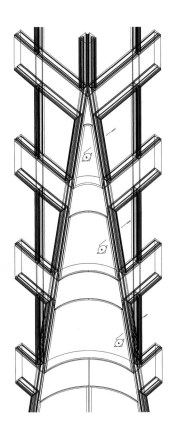

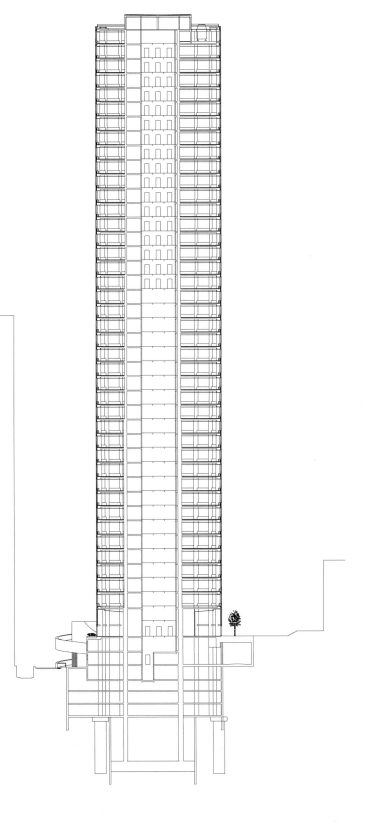

Transverse section

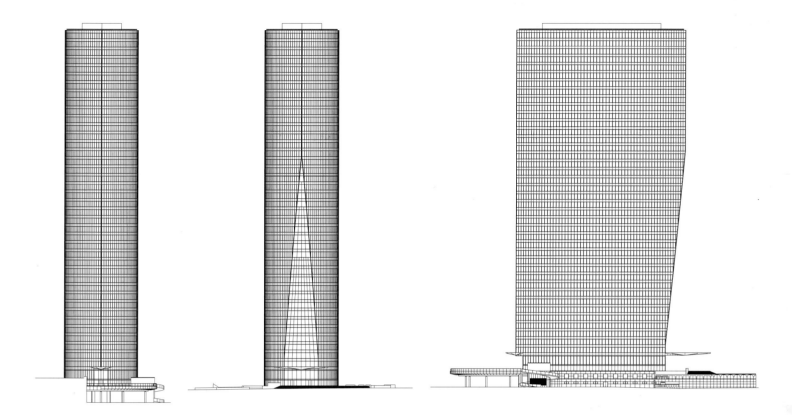

Elevations, rear, front, and side

Diagrams showing geometry of half-cone cutaway

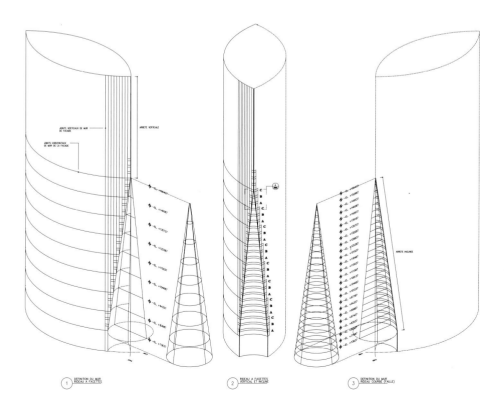

486 ft. (148 m)

Landmark Lofts

New York, New York
Project, 2001—03

Architect: Jean Nouvel | Ateliers Jean Nouvel

490 FEET (149 METERS) HIGH

The site for this project is an irregularly shaped block on the West Side of Manhattan in a low-rise area that has served as the borough's principal meat market and is now becoming a residential and commercial precinct that links established adjacent neighborhoods. The transitional character of the area can be seen in the shells of former commercial dock structures in the Hudson River just to the west of the property, in the existing older structures that occupy part of the polygonal site, and in the disused elevated freight railway bed that traverses it.

The design proposes a public park at ground level facing the river as a counterpoint to the tower, emphasizing the potential benefits of the transition from low-rise to high-rise occupancy by providing communal outdoor spaces. Other functions at ground level include commercial spaces under the bridge of the railway bed. At the second level, the diagonal axis of the railway bed, slated to become a public promenade connecting lower Manhattan with a midtown site for a proposed sports complex, is bounded by three distinct architectural forms. To the west is the tallest of these, a thirty-two story residential tower; mediating between this slender tower, with its relatively small floor plates of just over 4,000 square feet, and the existing low-rise structures to the east are a proposed nine-story block running parallel to the railway on its eastern edge and a proposed five-story triangular structure on the side of the tower. Restaurants and commercial spaces frame the proposed public walkway on the second level. At the sixth and ninth levels in the two taller structures, bridges span the elevated railway connecting units in both buildings and creating a Piranesi-like urban spatial drama.

The seemingly random fenestration of the tall metal-clad concrete structure derives from the essential condition of a tall building. As a relative condition, the height of Nouvel's tower provides for expansive views over and beyond the surrounding structures. The design of the residential units and the various window types and their placement enhances this condition. The placement of the windows also reflects the relationship of height to vision. As the floors ascend, the window openings are placed progressively lower with respect to average eye level. Just as the elevated railway threads public space through the development, connecting distant points in the city, the shifting heights of the window placement focus the view on the distant horizon.

The units tend to be loft-like with minimal intervening partitions between the interior spaces and the views out to the city and to the river. One window type has a sill and header angled upward to the exterior. A mirror on the sill turns the window into a kind of periscope to the sky. Another window type features jambs splayed toward the interior, creating expanded peripheral views. Yet another consists of an opening with a pivoting opaque panel, like a camera shutter, to allow the occupant to adjust the amount of light. The terraces are fitted with retractable glass walls in order to protect residents from the wind but not the view. These windscreens, on two of three sides of the protruding terraces, slide forward and back. Depending on the weather and the inclinations of the residents, the terraces give the facades a variety of configurations.

—Terence Riley

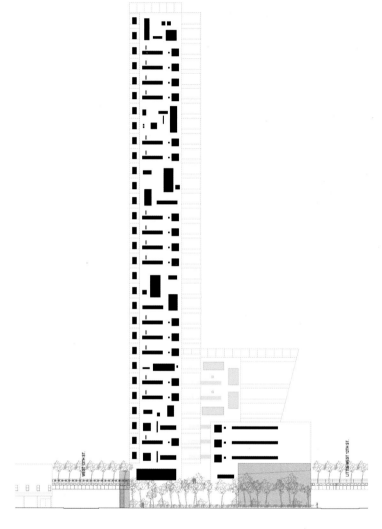

ABOVE Elevation
OPPOSITE View of south and east facades showing elevated railway bed (computer generated image)

490 ft. (149 m)

Plan, level 2

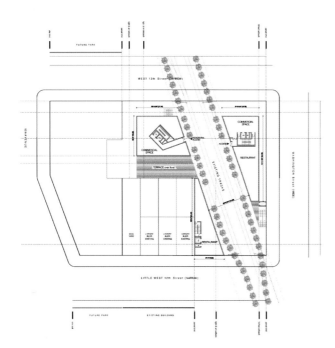

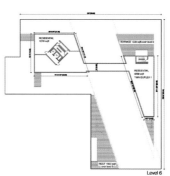

Plan, level 7

Plan, level 6

Ground-floor plan

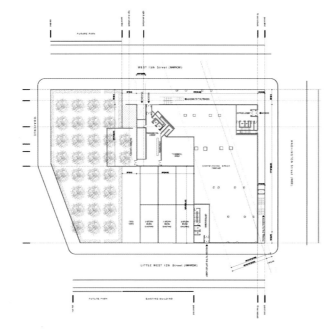

Site plan

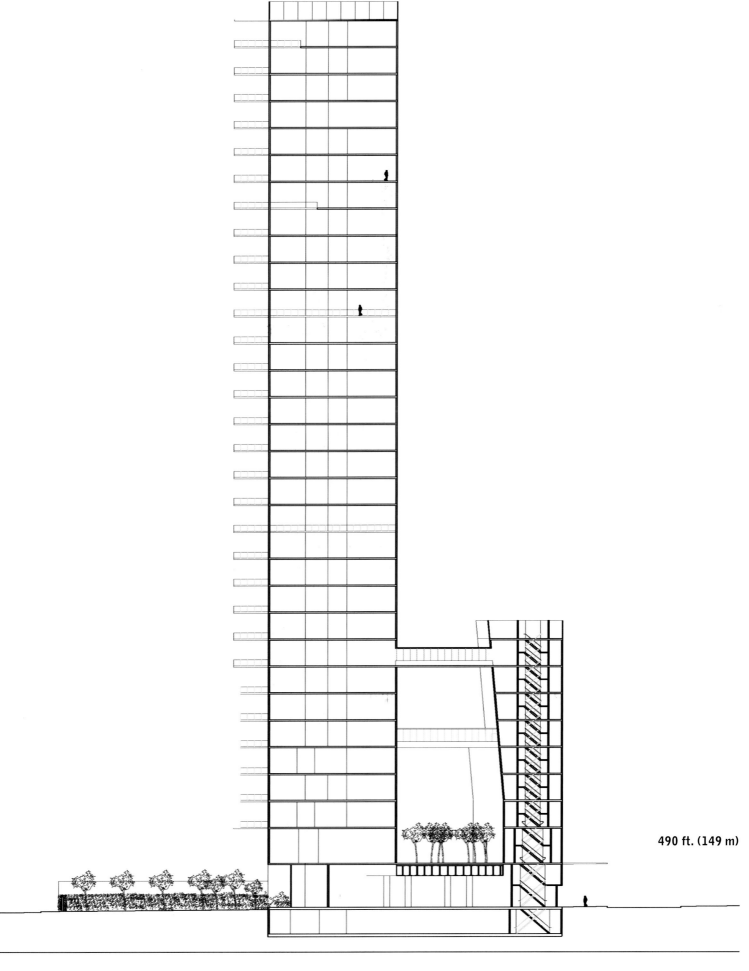

490 ft. (149 m)

Section, west-east

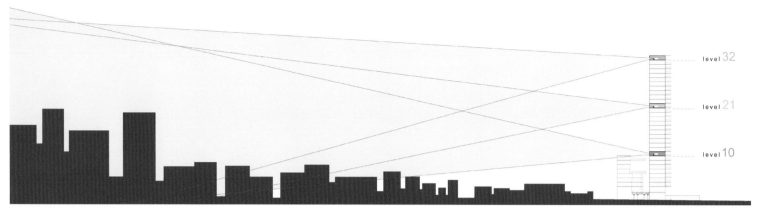

ABOVE Diagram of progressive lowering of window
placement according to eye level as building rises

level 32

level 21

level 10

mirror

mirror

internal elevation

metal cladding
insulation

exterior

interior

mirror cladding

plan

Reveals of windows angled and clad in mirror

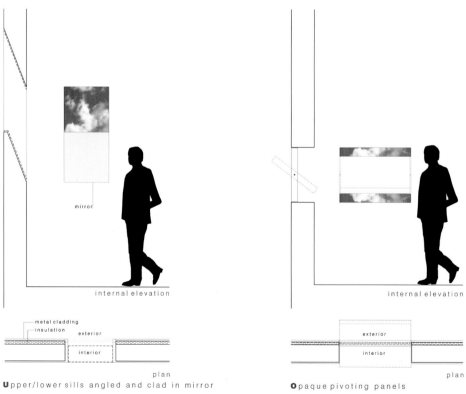

mirror

internal elevation

metal cladding
insulation

exterior

interior

plan

Upper/lower sills angled and clad in mirror

exterior

interior

internal elevation

plan

Opaque pivoting panels

RIGHT Diagrams showing window types
OPPOSITE View from west (computer generated
image)

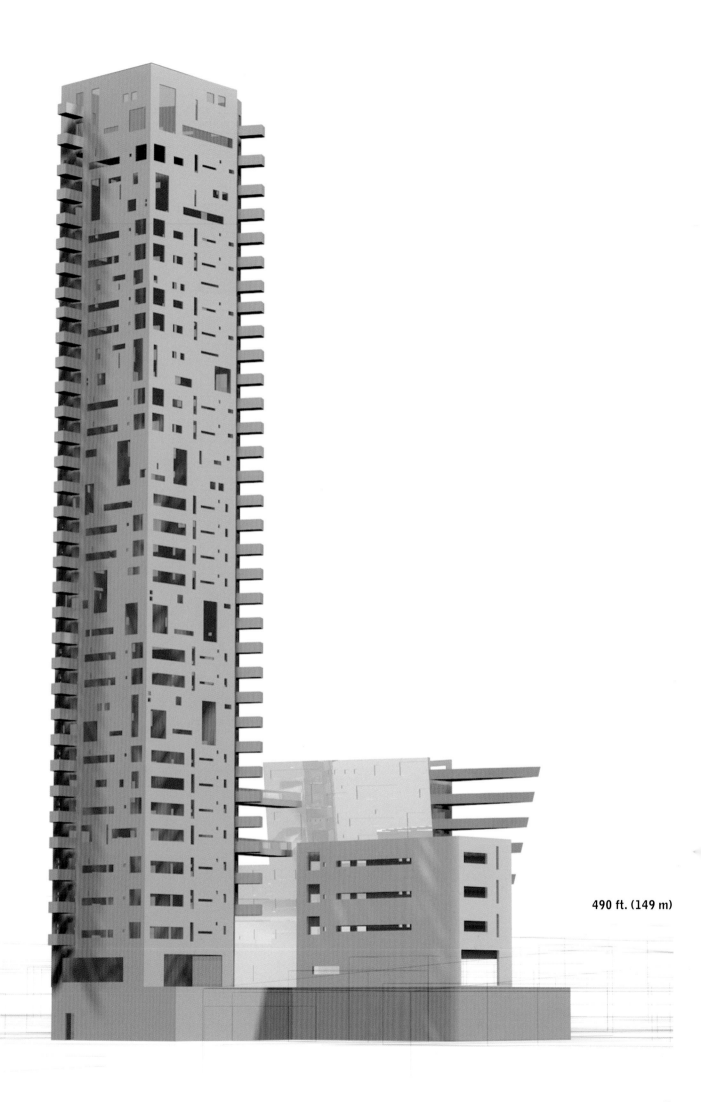

490 ft. (149 m)

Arcos Bosques Corporativo
Tower 1

Mexico City, Mexico
1993—96

Architects: Teodoro González de Léon, J. Francisco Serrano, Carlos Tejeda
Engineer: Alejandro Fierro Manly | Diseño y Supervision

530 FEET (162 METERS) HIGH

Arcos Bosques Corporativo's Tower 1 is the second stage in a six-stage master plan to construct the largest and most modern corporate office complex in Mexico. It is located at Bosques de las Lomas, an area in a western sector of Mexico City reclaimed for urban development in 1968. Conceived as a self-contained enclave, or urban retreat, where, in the architects' words, "a visitor … feels secluded, at rest in a serene environment," the master plan was the winning entry in a 1990 competition. While the original design included three identical arched towers, the final plan includes two, each 530 feet high, situated on sloping plinths. Four underground levels provide parking, and a massive curving wall of three six-story buildings delimits the complex. At its completion, the entire development will contain almost 2.5 million square feet of office space and a little more than 200,000 square feet of commercial and service space.

Tower I is constructed from identical fifteen-foot-square modules, each with a single ten-by-ten-foot window; on the facade these are consistently spaced five feet apart. Service cores have been allocated to the strong geometric volumes attached to the inner and outer side elevations of the arch—a parallelepiped and cylinders. Those along the outside of the tower provide services to the first eighteen floors, those on the inside to floors nineteen through thirty-four. The concrete facade, consisting of gravel, white-marble sand, and white cement, was hand-chiseled to expose the aggregate and to obtain a surface that tempers the strong Mexican light. The wedge-shaped base—a 30-60-90 triangle—has a grass-covered roof, seemingly an extension of the rural landscape beyond. Such a combination of surface, repetition, and rigorous geometry, plus the monumental columns in the lobby, produces a monolithic effect that echoes the texture and scale of ancient Mayan constructions.

The load-bearing facade walls measure two feet in thickness at the base and are as narrow as one foot at the top. The foundation consists of isolated footings for the four large interior columns and long footings for the facade columns and concrete walls. All footings are linked by tie beams. To construct the bridge of the arch, provisional steel structure supports were set on brackets at the twenty-seventh floor and then removed after the concrete pour of the first two floors of the arch. The steel and concrete floor of the bridge has additional horizontal bracing and extra reinforcement in the slab for earthquake resistance, although Bosques de las Lomas is outside the highly seismic central districts of Mexico City.

—Tina di Carlo

BELOW Northwest elevation and foundation plan
OPPOSITE View of Tower 1 from ground level

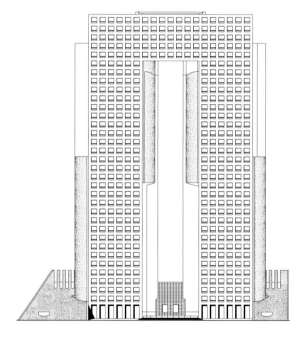

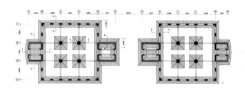

530 ft. (162 m)

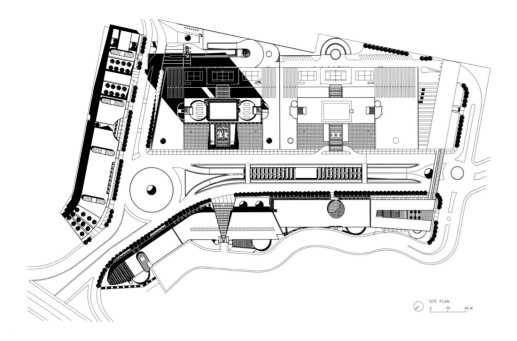

Site plan

View from the north

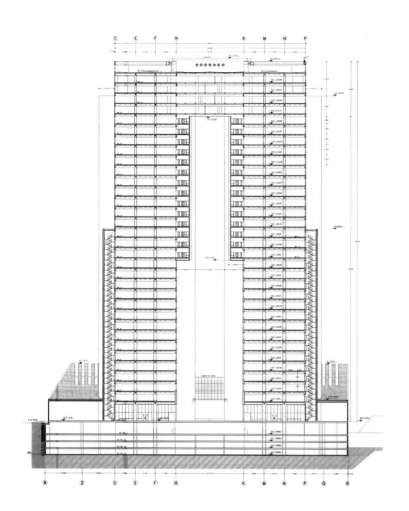

Longitudinal section, northeast–southwest

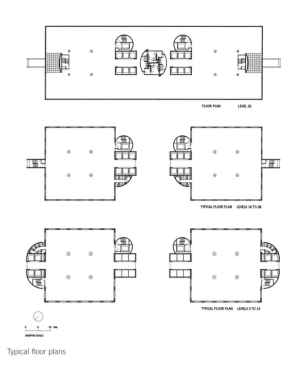

Typical floor plans

Transverse section, southeast–northwest

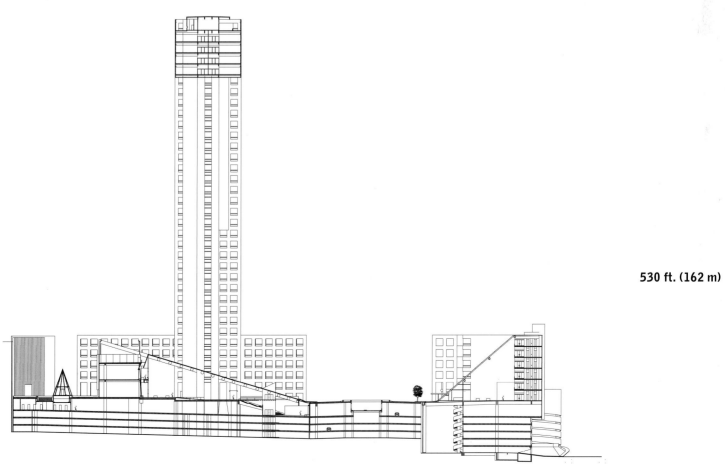

530 ft. (162 m)

Construction photograph

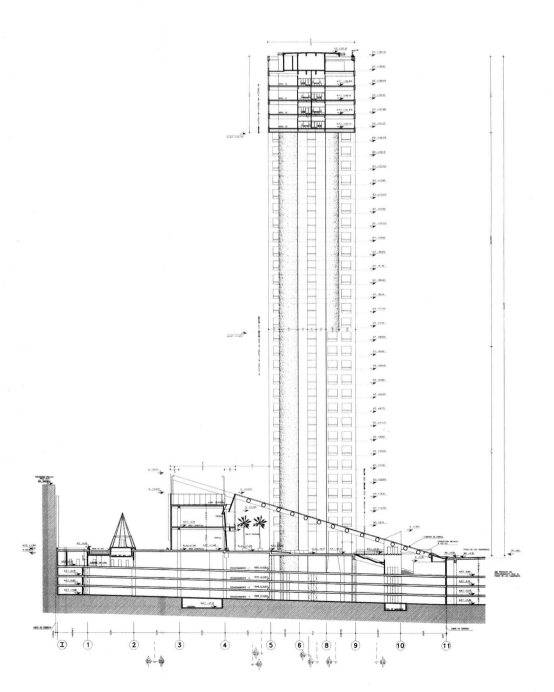

LEFT Transverse section, southeast–northwest
OPPOSITE Southwest elevation

530 ft. (162 m)

Fifth Avenue and Forty-second Street Tower

New York, New York
Project, 2002

Architect: Steven Holl | Steven Holl Architects
Engineers: Robert Silman, Nat Oppenheimer | Robert Silman Associates

585 FEET (178 METERS) HIGH

This tower was designed by Steven Holl to mark a critical intersection of two of Manhattan's most celebrated thoroughfares, Fifth Avenue and Forty-second Street. It rises over the northeast corner of this juncture, diagonally opposite the block occupied by the grand neoclassical New York Public Library, with its terraced front facade and its rear parterre garden, Bryant Park.

The diagonal axis between the vertical tower and the horizontally composed library and park is reinforced by Holl's structural and spatial solution for the building. It is a hybrid of concrete shear walls that stiffen the structure along the east and the north, making it read in plan "like an open book," and a lattice of steel columns and beams forming the curved glazed surfaces of the west and south facades.

Within the deep concrete walls' lateral zones, glass-backed elevators move up and down the blue-green zinc-paneled facades. These, along with other service elements, are visible from the north and east. From the elevator cabs, views up Fifth Avenue toward Central Park and east to Grand Central Station, the Chrysler Building, and the East River orient the viewer.

The complexity of the tower's glazed surface appears to be a gridded scrim wrapped over a still-life composition of stacked rectangles, cylinders, and other geometric forms. Beyond its monumental sculptural presence at a key crossroads, its somewhat mysterious forms can be read in a consistent way. At each point where the tower "warps" to a concave form—street level, the

ninth floor, and the apex—a public or semipublic space is created. At the street, this space becomes a place to survey the intersection itself with commercial space behind it. At the ninth and the thirty-sixth floors, terraces flow out from cafés overlooking the library and the park. From the upper-level café, spiraling ramps lead up to a "sky space," a spherical room conceived by the architect and the artist James Turrell.

The south and west orientations ensure that the glazed surfaces, embedded with photovoltaic, cells can generate enough power to illuminate the entire building with low-voltage fluorescent lights. At night, the sculptural form emits a glowing presence. The measurable scale of the glazing system gives the whole structure a human dimension that reads through its urban presence. Each of the glass panels is roughly the height of a passerby and has the proportions of 1:1.6, the relationship between the horizontal and vertical elements underlying many of the compositions of the ancient Greek architects and artists. The building as a whole can be read as a very metaphoric composition, with its open book and slouching man-about-town figure standing across the street from the magnificent library.

Holl's project recalls the importance of the tall building in creating urban identity, both in its dialogue with the immediate surroundings and in its place among the canyons of high-rises of Midtown Manhattan.

—Terence Riley

TOP Isometric sketch
BOTTOM Plan sketch
OPPOSITE Model, corner of Forty-second Street and Fifth Avenue

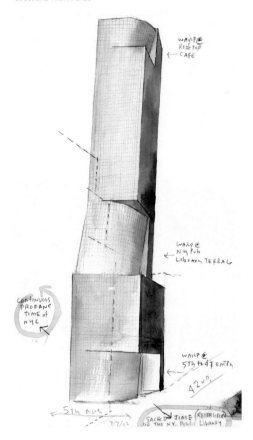

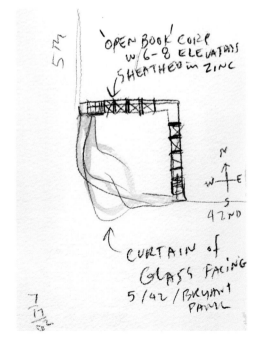

585 ft. (178 m)

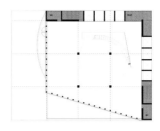

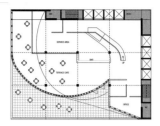

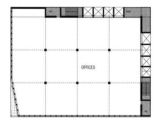

TOP TO BOTTOM

Typical plan, floors 16–35

Plan, library terrace café, floor 9

Typical plan, floors 5–8

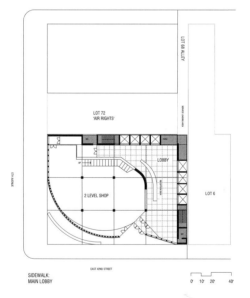

Site plan and ground-floor plan

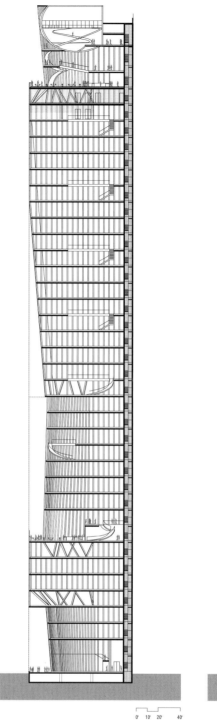

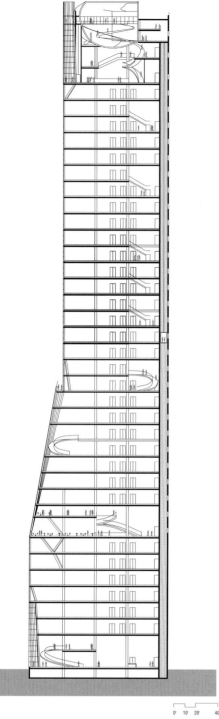

Sections, west–east

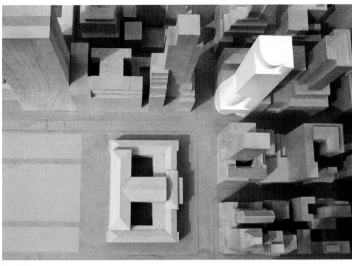

Model from above

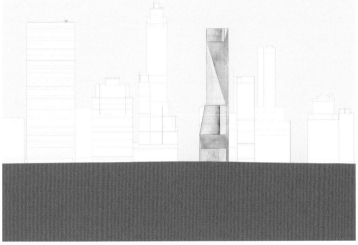

South elevation

BELOW Perspective sketch of entry looking
southwest toward New York Public Library
RIGHT View looking northeast across Fifth
Avenue from New York Public Library
(computer-generated image)

585 ft. (178 m)

30 St. Mary Axe
Swiss Reinsurance Headquarters

London, England
Design, 1997–2000; projected completion, 2004

Architect: Norman Foster | Foster and Partners
Engineer: John Brazier | Ove Arup & Partners

590 FEET (180 METERS) HIGH

The new forty-story Swiss Reinsurance Headquarters in London is circular in plan on a rectilinear site within a dense urban fabric. This allows for extensive public space around the tower, which flows directly into the structure's first two stories of retail spaces, reiterating the circulation motif of the tower itself.

The circumference of the building changes as the tower rises: it expands from a 162-foot-diameter footprint at ground level to a maximum diameter of 185 feet at the seventeenth floor and then tapers to its crown, a double-height entertainment and dining facility with 360-degree views of the city for the use of the building's occupants.

Unlike traditional buildings using vertical supports, this one is designed so that the principal structural elements are a central circular core and a "diagrid" of diagonally interlocking steel elements that spiral upward around the outer edge of the tower and meet at the apex. Horizontal hoops at every other floor complete the perimeter structure, creating a very stiff triangulated shell. The aerodynamic form of the building, in plan and in the tapering vertical profile, reduces the downward wash of turbulent wind gusts that often exists around tall buildings in urban settings. The form of the building also enhances some of the negative environmental effects of tall buildings by dispersing reflected light and deflecting gusting winds.

Without the need for intervening columns, the office spaces between the self-supporting core and the outer structural shell are completely open. Six triangular light-wells, symmetrically arranged, pierce each circular floor plate, increasing the amount of daylight that reaches into the building and allowing visual communication between floors. Each floor plate is then rotated slightly so that the six light wells do not stack vertically to create long shafts but spiral around the surface of the building following the shifting modules of the "diagrid."

The inventive structural design of the Swiss Reinsurance Headquarters is matched by its mechanical systems. In addition to creating a sense of community through visual communication, the spiraling light wells also conduct fresh air upward through the building. For forty percent of the year, air pressure differentials created by the building's aerodynamic form can serve to move the air, greatly reducing energy consumption. The requirements for cooling the building are also greatly diminished by its double-glazed skin. Solar heat gain is dissipated in the airspace between the two layers of glass and thrust upward and out before it enters the building. Warm air within the building is also drawn into the airspace and out of the office environment.

This ambitious environmental model comes very close to realizing R. Buckminster Fuller's description of his Climatroffice project of the 1970s, "a micro-climate within an energy-conscious envelope." The interlacing of architectural, mechanical, and structural design would not have been possible without the parametric modeling used by the aerospace and automotive industries to generate complex systems and forms. The remarkable technical innovations of the Swiss Reinsurance Headquarters spring from various sources and tools outside of traditional architectural practice, and far beyond the practices of real-estate development markets. While creating higher initial costs, the innovative design insures long-term gains.

—Terence Riley

BELOW Conceptual sketches of airflow
OPPOSITE View from street (computer-generated image)

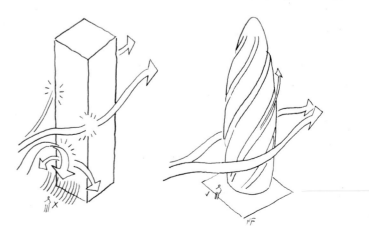

590 ft. (180 m)

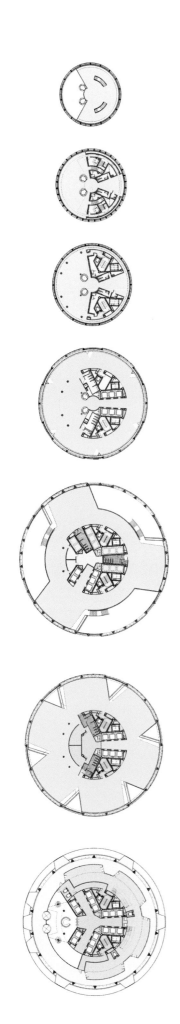

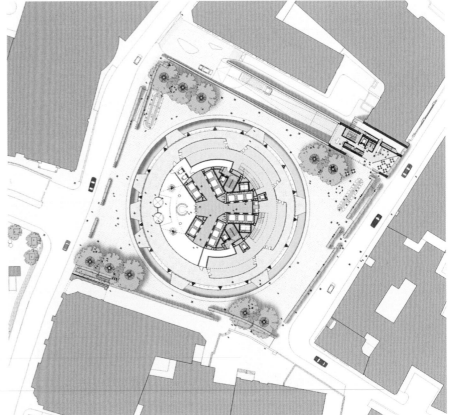

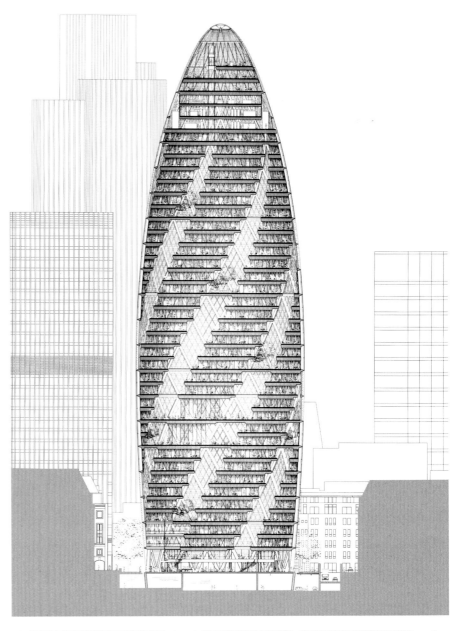

ABOVE Typical floor plans from ground floor to upper levels
TOP RIGHT Section, east–west
BOTTOM RIGHT Site plan

ABOVE View from south bank of the Thames
(computer-generated image)

RIGHT Model from above

590 ft. (180 m)

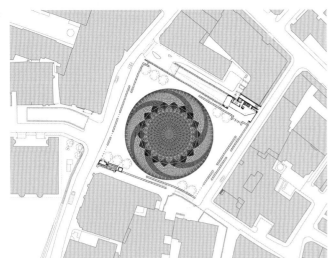

Roof plan

View looking northeast

The "city grid" is really a 4 storey increment, visually

The "City within a City" has always been full of surprises !

Perspective sketch

View of light well under construction

Facade detail showing "diagrid"

590 ft. (180 m)

Construction photograph

Detail model of light wells

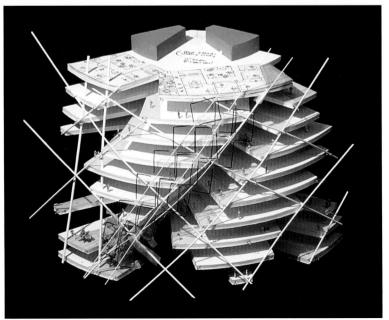

Construction photograph

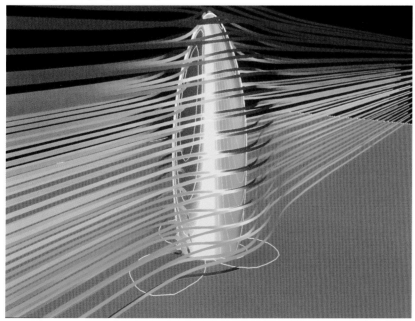

Wind-flow diagram (computer-generated image)

590 ft. (180 m)

New York Times Headquarters

New York, New York
Project, 2000

Architects: Frank O. Gehry | Gehry Partners; David Childs | Skidmore,
    Owings & Merrill
Engineers: William F. Baker, Hal Iyengar | Skidmore, Owings & Merrill

606 FEET (185 METERS) HIGH

In 2000, the New York Times sponsored a competition for a tall building that would be its headquarters. The architects invited to participate were Renzo Piano, Norman Foster, and a team that included Frank O. Gehry and David Childs.

The site for the new building runs along Eighth Avenue between Fortieth and Forty-first streets in Manhattan. The competition brief called for a structure of approximately 1.5 million square feet, half of which was to be occupied by the New York Times and half rented to tenants.

As submitted, Gehry's design is a forty-three-story tower ringed at street level by retail space; the entry at street level is also a multi-height hall that brings visitors below grade to additional levels of retail space as well as links to the subway. The novel and dramatic application of Gehry's unorthodox geometries, familiar to those who know his work, to a tall building invigorates the formal language of the project. The design is sculptural in its overall effect, but the aesthetic dimension does not overwhelm the building's urban legibility. At street level, the facades seem to peel and unfurl, creating canopies to protect passersby and signifying the location of the principal entrance. The unfolding of the building's form at this level also breaks the mass of the tower

into smaller elements, in keeping with nearby urban patterns. The structure proposed by William F. Baker is a simple frame that punctuates the interior space with its geometric configuration.

As the midsection of the tower rises, it accommodates the large horizontal floor plates necessary for the New York Times operations, the heart of which is a 170,000-square-foot newsroom visible from the newspaper's lobby. Above the tower's midsection, the surfaces begin to curve and fold, setting back to meet the city's zoning laws as well as creating smaller floor plates for rental tenants. In the uppermost floors, the tower splits into multiple sections, creating a crown that, like the Chrysler Building and many other New York skyscrapers, gives it an identity within the overall urban skyline. The undulating forms at the apex are reminiscent of the flowing gothic script of the New York Times logo, which is imprinted upon the glazed surface.

Part of the inventiveness of the tower is in its associations to earlier architecture, such as Louis Sullivan's fusion of post-and-lintel construction with organic decorative detail and Adolf Loos's conception of the skyscraper as a three-part composition of pedestal, shaft, and capital.

—Terence Riley

BELOW Sketch
OPPOSITE Model, southwest corner
along Eighth Avenue

606 ft. (185 m)

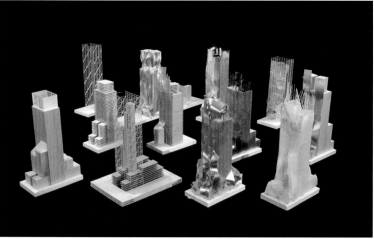

TOP Study model with skyline
BOTTOM Twelve study models

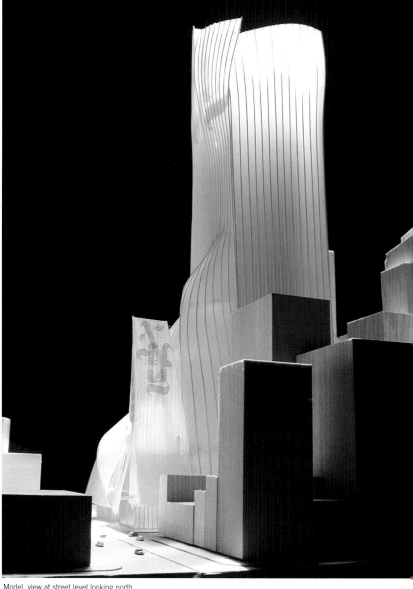

Model, view at street level looking north
along Eighth Avenue

TOP TO BOTTOM
Plan, floor 40
Plan, floor 18
Plan, floor 6

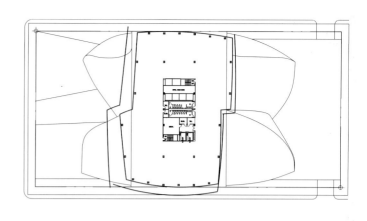

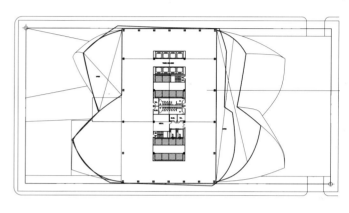

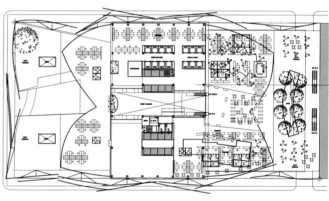

Site plan and ground-floor plan

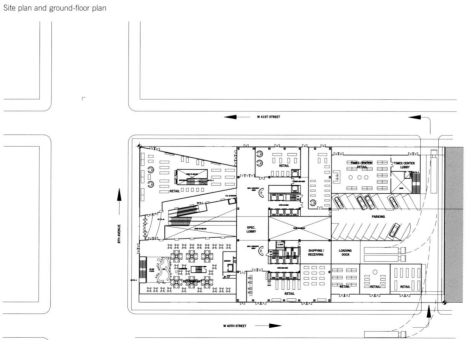

606 ft. (185 m)

TOP Detail model of lobby and atrium
BOTTOM Detail model of escalators from
ground floor to lobby

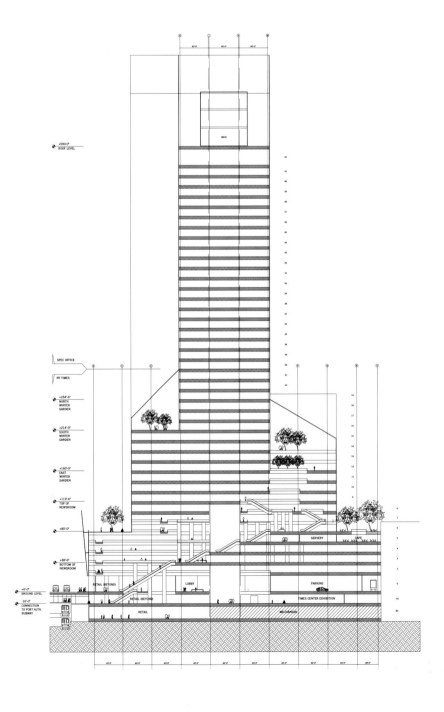

Section, west–east

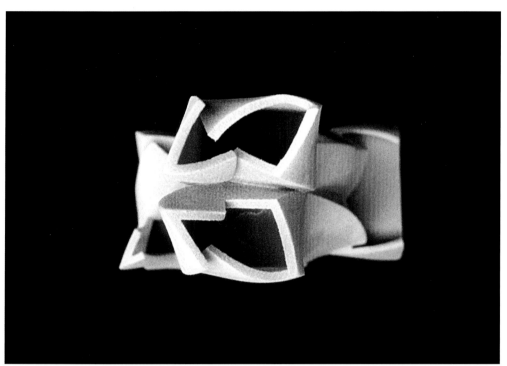

TOP Study model from above
BOTTOM Study model

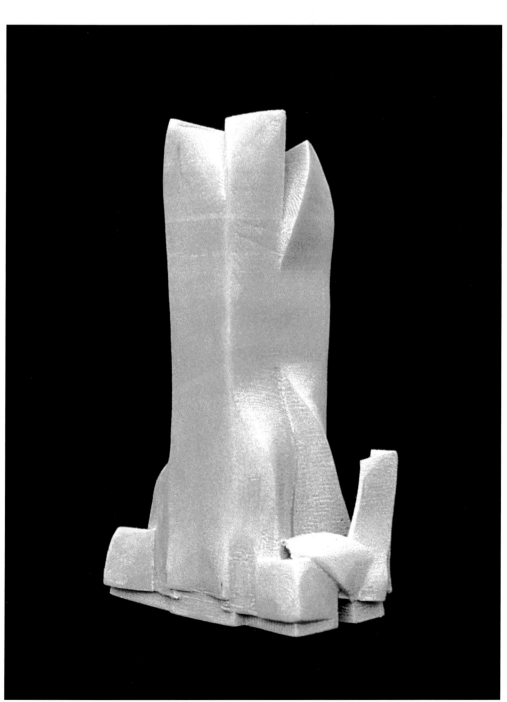

606 ft. (185 m)

Turning Torso
Apartment and Office Tower

Malmö, Sweden
Design, 1999—2001; projected completion, 2005

Architect: Santiago Calatrava
Engineer: Santiago Calatrava

623 FEET (190 METERS) HIGH

Santiago Calatrava's Turning Torso, a mixed-use tower of office and residential space, reflects what he calls the universal structural law dictated by all natural forms, namely, that the base is thicker than the crown. On a footprint slightly smaller than one hundred feet in diameter, nine five-sided, five-story volumes rotate a total of ninety degrees over a rise of 523 feet. The core, made of reinforced concrete, provides wind resistance and encloses vertical circulation: three high-speed elevators, staircases, and mechanical shafts. While its interior radius remains a constant sixteen and one-half feet, the thickness of its wall radically slims from eight feet at the base to one and one-quarter feet at the top.

The structure is further reinforced by a steel truss, or "exoskeleton"—an external frame consisting of a columnar tension spine situated at the edges of the triangular extensions of the five-sided volumes, to which a series of horizontal and diagonal rib-like struts is attached. The exoskeleton is then tied to a large anchored-pile foundation slab, which provides additional lateral stability. The combination of compressive core and tension spine creates a sense of dynamism in the form.

The central core is anchored to a foundation nearly one hundred feet in diameter and nearly fifty feet deep, which lifts the nine volumes, or approximately 23,000-square-foot sub-buildings, two stories off the ground to form an exposed basement. The first twelve stories provide approximately 43,000 square feet of office space; the upper thirty-eight levels are strictly residential. A hotel and gym are provided on the forty-third floor. Each floor can be divided into five separate dwellings with common areas such as meeting rooms, saunas, and gyms allocated to the triangular areas between the five-sided vol-

ume and the vertical spine of the exoskeleton. The spaces between each sub-building are intended for use as observation decks. All wet areas, including bathrooms, kitchens, and laundry areas are adjacent to the core. A secondary adjacent structure provides parking, shops, and restaurants.

Turning Torso was initially designed for Sweden's 2001 housing exposition in Malmö: *BoO1—City of Tomorrow.* The exposition was initiated because Malmö, a small port located on Sweden's southwestern tip, was facing a rapid rise in housing demands with the opening of the Oresund Bridge linking Sweden to mainland Europe in 2000. Calatrava's tower proposes a sustainable solution to provide the much-needed housing. It uses the Western Harbor of Malmö's green-wind energy, supplied from a nearby windmill. Solar panels on the roof of the adjacent garage building supply electricity to light the corridors. Construction time is minimized by the use of slip-form, or sliding, formwork to cast the central concrete core. Each set of five floor plates per volume is to be poured in place, spliced to the central core, and supported from below by inclined perimeter columns. The steel exoskeleton and white facade elements, and the glass and painted aluminum, will all be prefabricated off-site to minimize construction time.

Situated at the intersection of two roads, the tower enhances a windy previously derelict public area of Malmö. As the only vertical element in an otherwise low-lying terrain it has become, even before its completion, an iconic presence in the landscape, at once echoing the twisting modular rhythms of the human body, yet reversing the paradigm by placing the skeleton outside the skin.

—Tina di Carlo

BELOW Watercolor sketch
OPPOSITE Model from above

623 ft. (190 m)

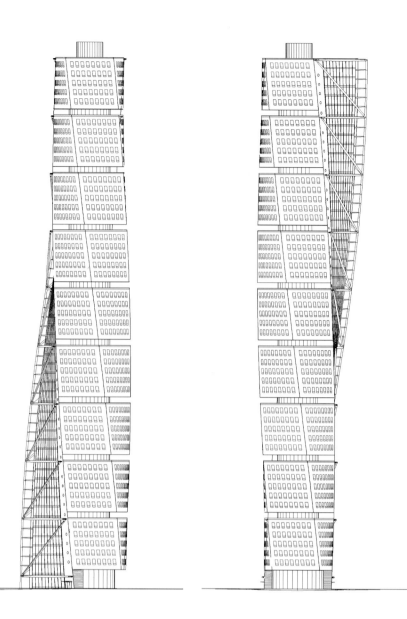

Elevations

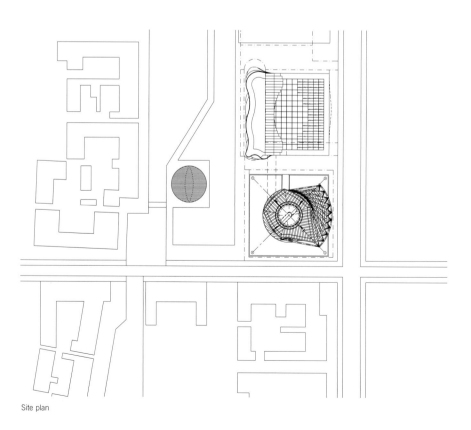

Site plan

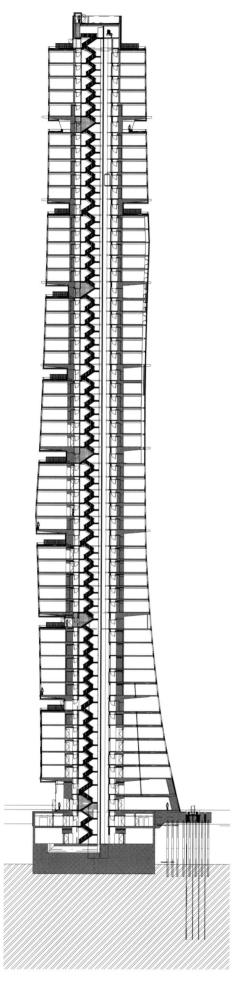

Section, east–west

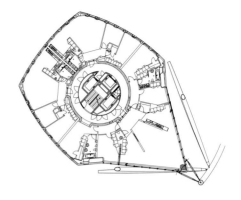

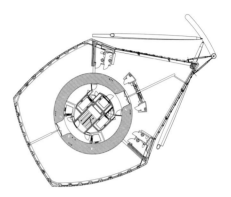

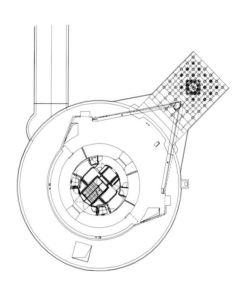

TOP TO BOTTOM:
Plan, floor 50
Plan, floor 2
Ground-floor plan

623 ft. (190 m)

Construction photographs showing foundation and core

View in Malmö

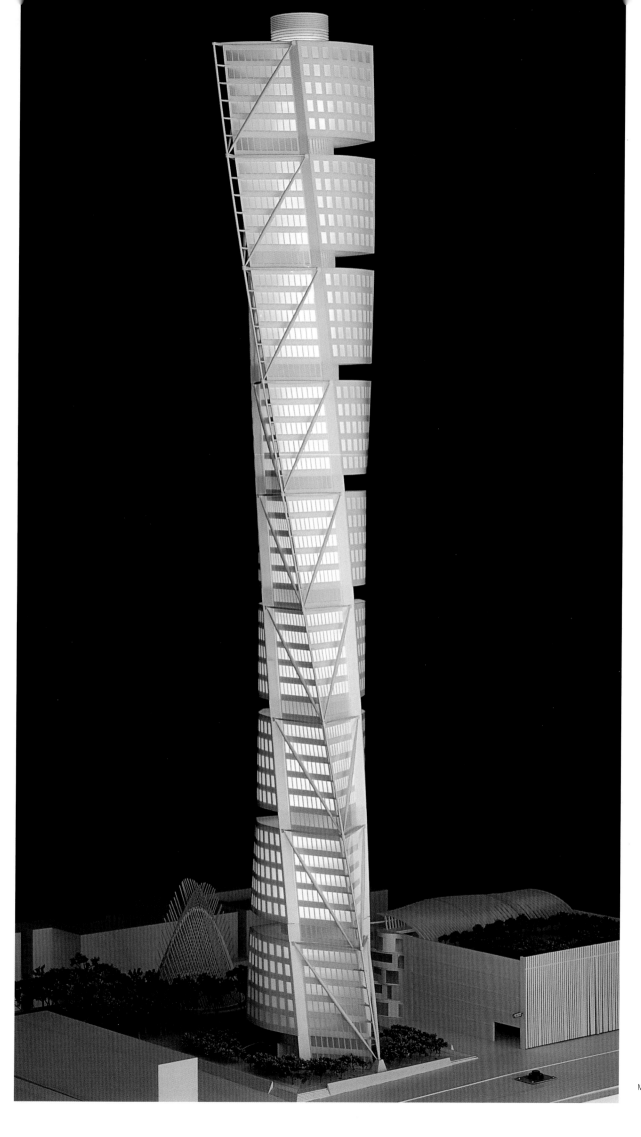

623 ft. (190 m)

Model

Industrialized Housing System

Korea
Project, 1991–92

Architect: Richard Rogers | Richard Rogers Partnership
Engineer: Ove Arup & Partners

660 FEET (201 METERS) HIGH

In 1991, the Korean manufacturer Hanseem Corporation, responded to the rapidly increasing demand for affordable housing in Korea by commissioning Richard Rogers Partnership to research the design and manufacture of a high-quality, low-cost housing system. The ultimate objective was to make 100,000 fully furnished units at twenty percent of the conventional cost.

Through the use of up-to-date materials and techniques, the architect, in close collaboration with Ove Arup & Partners, proposed an environmentally conscious, repetitive system for low-cost manufacturing to produce both diverse architectural forms and also individualized living spaces. He believed that an innovative method of production, relying on engineering as well as architecture, would result in substantial savings.

The Industrial Housing System essentially comprised a kit of parts (a concept often used in industrial design but here applied to architecture): foundation, column, structural unit, glazed unit, staircase, and balcony that could be assembled in various configurations. These components, manufactured and fitted off-site, could be transported via truck to various locations throughout Korea. The modules could then be assembled at any site, including those on the steep hills that make up much of the Korean landscape, as single dwellings or in low- or high-rise configurations. The modular nature of the units would facilitate automated construction: installation would be carried out by computer-controlled cranes, much like those used to stack containers in ships, which read magnetically coded "stripes" placed on the units while they are still in the factory, significantly boosting the rate of production and eliminating human error.

Modular units would range from 139 to 837 square feet and could accommodate a single person or a family. In order to provide for specific needs, the layout of each unit could be designed individually, the modular interior enabling customers to start with a basic model and add units, increasing fitting options with different levels of equipment. Whether built gradually or at one time, each unit is an arrangement of specific modular pieces allowing for a wide variety of design options within.

The configuration could be reviewed on a computer-generated model prior to shipment, a progressive method in the early 1990s, thus eliminating costly post-construction alterations. In addition to expected services, such as heating, lighting, and air conditioning, the units incorporate systems for security, communications, information, and entertainment. All interior fittings are installed before the modules are transported to their final location.

An environmentally friendly program, the project would rely on high-performance, low-energy mechanical and electrical systems incorporating natural sources for heat and light. On-site assembly would have minimal impact on the landscape. The units' unique lightweight structural panel system would be made from composites of recycled plastic and sheet metals, a low-cost system capable of supporting high direct loads.

Rogers's interest in structurally innovative, flexible, and cost-efficient solutions to mass housing exists within a tradition of such modernist work as the architect/engineer R. Buckminster Fuller's Dymaxion House project (1927–29), which sought to adapt assembly-line automotive production methods to make a house at the same cost as a car. Other designers, including Le Corbusier and Frank Lloyd Wright, have also explored systems for affordable comfortable housing using factory-based prefabrication. This Industrial Housing System also recalls the "plug-in" concept of architecture explored by Peter Cook and Archigram, the visionary British counterculture group of the 1960s.

—Bevin Cline

BELOW Diagrams of assembled units
OPPOSITE View looking northeast

ASSEMBLED UNITS

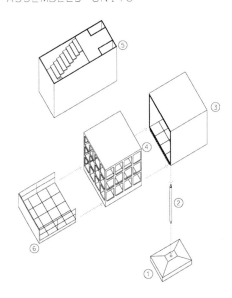

1. FOUNDATIONS 4. GLAZED UNIT
2. COLUMNS 5. STAIRCASE
3. STRUCTURAL UNIT 6. BALCONY

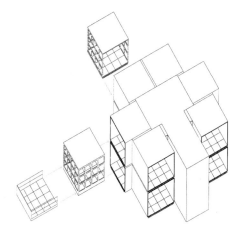

660 ft. (201 m)

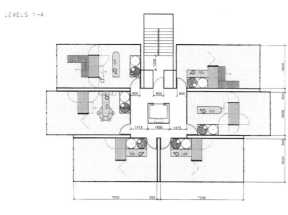

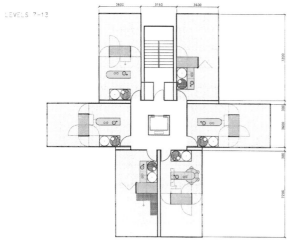

FLOOR PLANS

LEFT Typical plans, floors 1–4, 7–13
BELOW Site plan

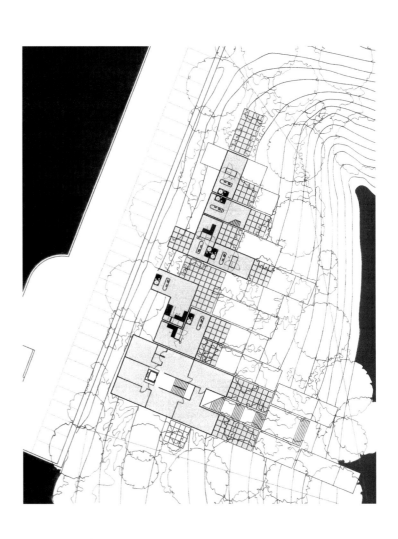

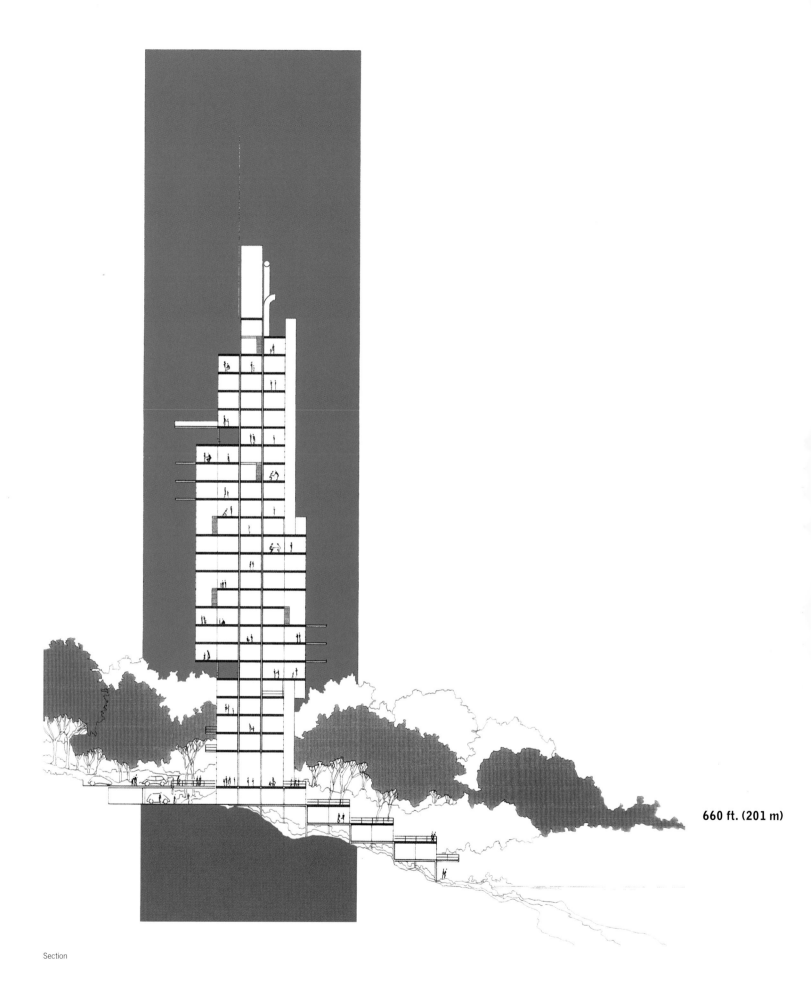

660 ft. (201 m)

Section

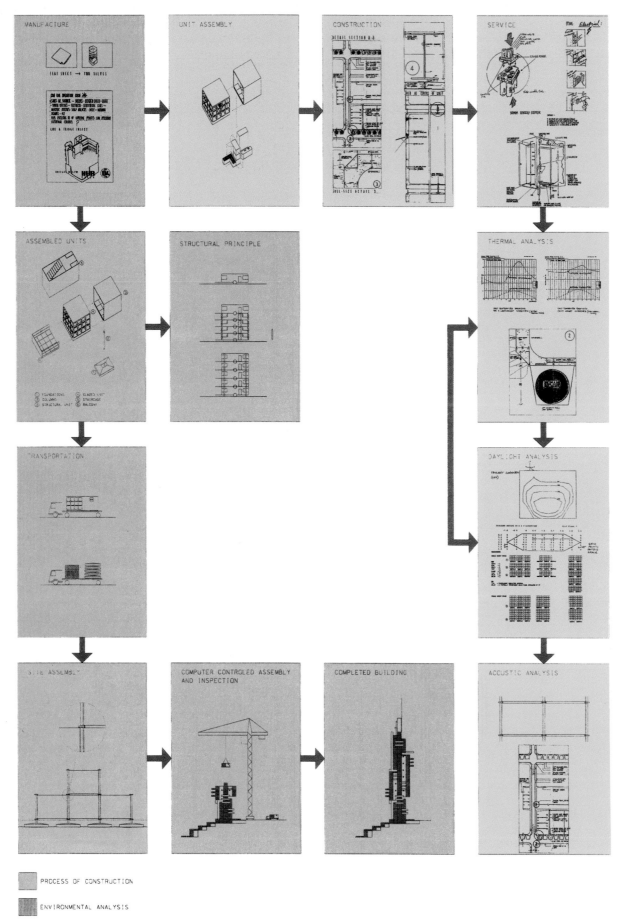

MANUFACTURE

UNIT ASSEMBLY

CONSTRUCTION

SERVICE

ASSEMBLED UNITS

STRUCTURAL PRINCIPLE

THERMAL ANALYSIS

TRANSPORTATION

DAYLIGHT ANALYSIS

SITE ASSEMBLY

COMPUTER CONTROLED ASSEMBLY AND INSPECTION

COMPLETED BUILDING

ACCUSTIC ANALYSIS

PROCESS OF CONSTRUCTION

ENVIRONMENTAL ANALYSIS

ABOVE Construction and environmental-analysis diagram
OPPOSITE View looking west

660 ft. (201 m)

122 Leadenhall Street

London, England
Project, 2002–03

Architect: Richard Rogers | Richard Rogers Partnership
Engineer: David Glover | Ove Arup & Partners

728 FEET (222 METERS) HIGH

The tower at 122 Leadenhall Street by Richard Rogers is located in the center of the City of London, adjacent to St. Helen's Square, to Norman Foster's new Swiss Reinsurance Headquarters, and to Rogers's own building for Lloyd's of London (1986). The tower's wedge-shaped form allows it to maximize and preserve light at the street level and on the interior, while respecting the immediate context, the London skyline, and a key local view of St. Paul's Cathedral from Fleet Street. The forty-seven-story tower, in which the floor plates diminish as the building rises, will provide almost one million square feet of office space, in addition to retail and public spaces at the ground level.

Unlike traditional tall structures with interior service cores, this tower's service core does not lie at the center of the building in order to offer lateral stability; rather, the mechanical systems, elevators, stairs, and sanitary facilities have been allocated to an exterior zone attached to the northern facade of the building. A truss system, or perimeter braced "mega-frame" tube, provides lateral stability. This externally expressed structure is visible on the east, west, and south facades; on the north facade, it is situated between the office area and service core. The triangular-shaped facades to the east and west support a "diagrid" of inclined columns that absorbs both horizontal and vertical loads. This efficient design leaves the office space and core zones generally free of any bracing structures and columns. In fact, only four columns support the long-span lightweight composite floors of steel and concrete at the lower levels; the columns eventually disappear as the floors recede. The large, relatively column-free floors in combination with the tapering form allow for maximum flexibility—either modular office or open

plan—while maximizing views toward the Thames and daylight. Four elevators service the lower floors, and the mid-level and upper-floor sectors each have eight apiece, making a total of twenty elevators. Future plans include a low-energy design of environmentally sound materials and modular construction. A facade that limits solar gains and minimizes glare will control heat absorption and allow the use of a number of low-energy air-conditioning systems, such as chilled beams or ceilings.

While the site measures roughly 220 by 165 feet, the tower's footprint is considerably smaller, occupying roughly half of the site. The first floor is cut back to provide a canopy and platform over the raked ground-floor level, and permits the outdoor public space to flow into the lobby of the building. Flanking escalators bring occupants to the second level, where they can enter the service core directly to the north of the structure. The overall geometry of the placement of the building on the site, along with the setback first floor (and cantilevering of the subsequent five), preserves and enhances the green pedestrian network characteristic of London in the north–south direction and creates a significant east–west pedestrian axis. For the architect, this strategy "pulls the mass of the building off Leadenhall Street."

The design exemplifies Rogers's contention that the implementation of sustainability and the preservation of the city square are paramount to the vitality of city life. This premise can be seen in Rogers's work as far back as the Centre Georges Pompidou, which he designed in collaboration with Renzo Piano in 1977, where half of the site was given over to an urban square.
—Tina di Carlo

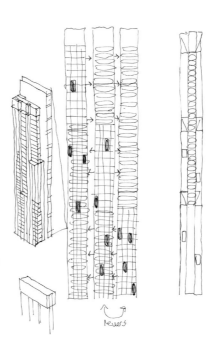

Sketch

View of southeast corner
(computer-generated image)

728 ft. (222 m)

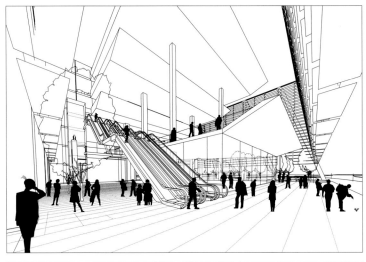

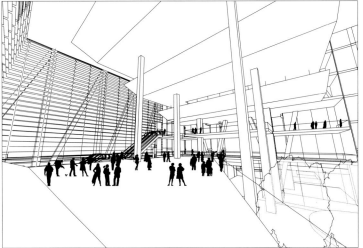

ABOVE Perspectives of ground-floor lobby

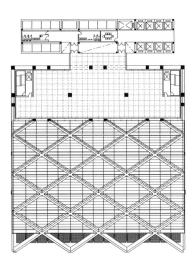

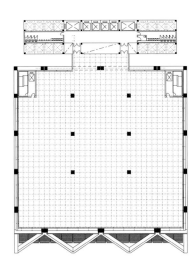

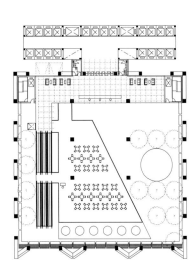

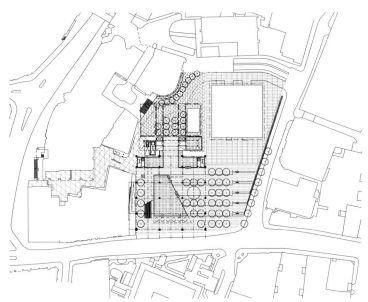

Site plan

TOP TO BOTTOM
Plan, floor 45
Plan, floor 5
Ground-floor plan

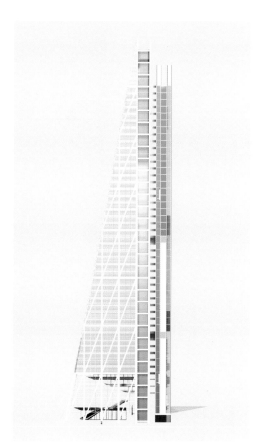

East elevation (computer-generated image)

North elevation (computer-generated image)

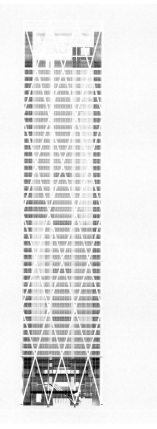

South elevation (computer-generated image)

Transverse section, north–south

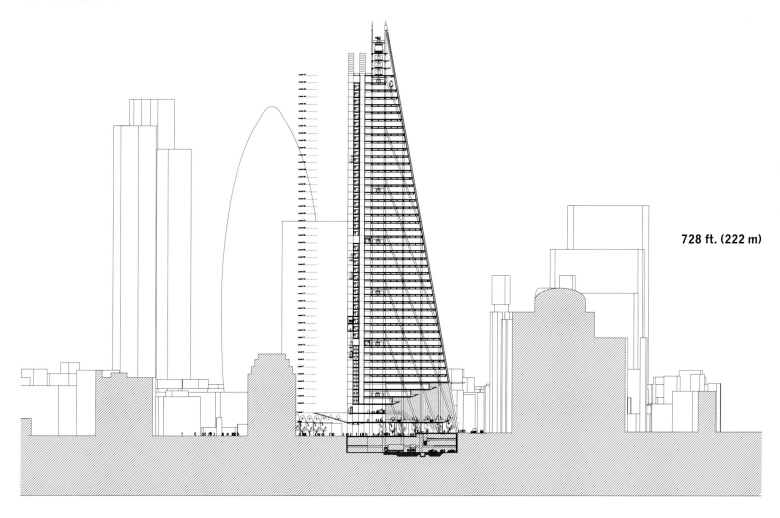

728 ft. (222 m)

Central Chinese Television (CCTV) Tower

Beijing, China
Design, 2002–04; projected completion, 2008

Architects: Rem Koolhaas, Ole Scheeren | Office for Metropolitan Architecture
Engineers: Cecil Balmond, Craig Gibbons, Michael Kwok, Rory McGowan | Ove Arup & Partners

768 FEET (234 METERS) HIGH

View of front facade (computer-generated image)

The proposed new headquarters for the Central Chinese Television Corporation is to be built on a twenty-five-acre site in Beijing's new central business district, along a major axis east of the Imperial Palace. The approximately 4,360,000-square-foot headquarters building is remarkable not for its height but for its form, which rises, cantilevers, and descends in a continuous loop. The building's central cavity, or "window" opening, frames an adjacent 1,250,000-square-foot cultural center, which is also part of the project, as is the surrounding media park.

The headquarters building houses administration, news, broadcasting, studio, and production facilities. The continuous loop suggests the flow of work from the production areas to the recording studios to the broadcast areas, an assembly line for international media, rather than a top-down structure that emphasizes corporate hierarchy. In the words of the architect: "The consolidation of the television program in a single building allows each worker to be permanently aware of his co-workers—a chain of interdependence that promotes solidarity rather than isolation, collaboration instead of opposition. The building itself contributed to the coherence of the organization."

The looping configuration also serves as a model for the mechanical systems. Heating, ventilation, and cooling systems thread through the structure like arteries in the body. Sequential elevator banks rise vertically then step laterally through the canted volumes.

The greatest challenge of the design of the building is the structural system. Conceived as a continuous tube, with the principal supporting elements in the surface of the loop, the volume was first projected with a uniform diagonal grid wrapped about its surface. The grid was then analyzed using an iterative computer-based method to establish zones of stress for the diagonal members, from lowest to highest. In areas of greatest stress, the density of the triangulated members was increased and/or members were deformed to respond more precisely to the lateral and dead loads. In the areas where the uniform triangulation was providing more support than was required, redundant members were removed or deformed to allow for greater stresses elsewhere. The result is an efficient and reliable structure for revisiting earthquakes as well. The cantilever overhang requires additional support in the form of a two-story-deep truss at the lower level of the overhang, which transfers its load to the perimeter tube and to the foundation level.

The stability of the structural tube is evident in the planned method of construction, wherein the construction of the structural skin precedes the completion of the lower floors and the cores. When complete, the surface will be a rich texture of the deformed diagonal grid with a glazed skin imbedded with images representing a kind of international sign language of the media age: a handshake, a computer, and other iconic images and text.

Adolf Loos's famous rendering of the skyscraper as a monumental classical column, with base, shaft, and capital, and Louis Sullivan's metaphor of the tall building as a honeycomb of cellular units have long served as metaphors for the tall building, endlessly re-interpreted. The CCTV headquarters is one of the first high-rise buildings to suggest a new paradigm, one that creates urban space instead of simply displacing it, capturing the urban space into a kind of hybrid public/private condition—a sculptural effect in the tradition of urban ensembles such as Rockefeller Center.

—Terence Riley

768 ft. (234 m)

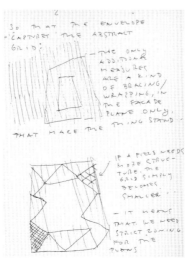

Sketches

View within Beijing (computer-generated image)

Section

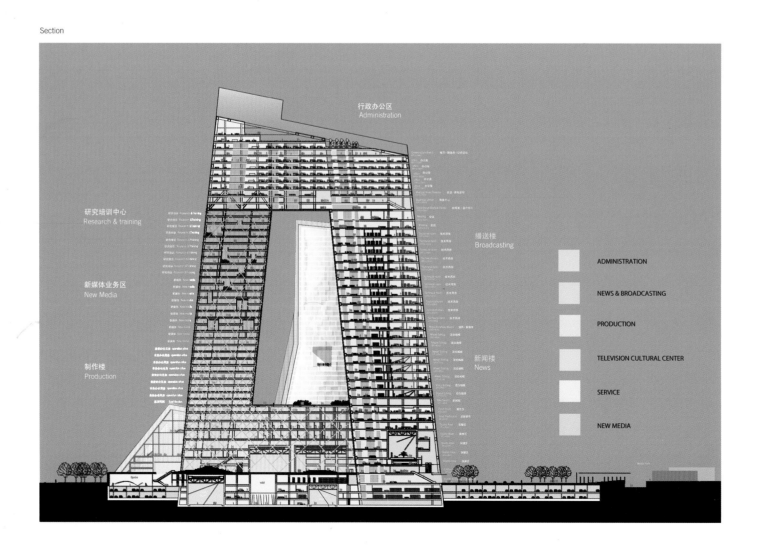

行政办公区
Administration

研究培训中心
Research & training

播送楼
Broadcasting

新媒体业务区
New Media

新闻楼
News

制作楼
Production

ADMINISTRATION

NEWS & BROADCASTING

PRODUCTION

TELEVISION CULTURAL CENTER

SERVICE

NEW MEDIA

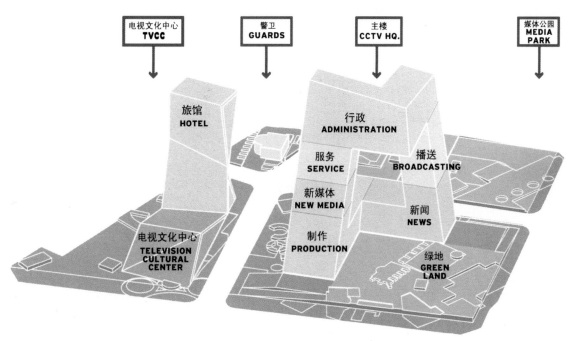

电视文化中心 TVCC	警卫 GUARDS	主楼 CCTV HQ.	媒体公园 MEDIA PARK

旅馆 HOTEL

行政 ADMINISTRATION

服务 SERVICE

播送 BROADCASTING

新媒体 NEW MEDIA

新闻 NEWS

制作 PRODUCTION

电视文化中心 TELEVISION CULTURAL CENTER

绿地 GREEN LAND

Diagram of programmatic distribution

Facade detail

768 ft. (234 m)

Overhead view (computer-generated image)

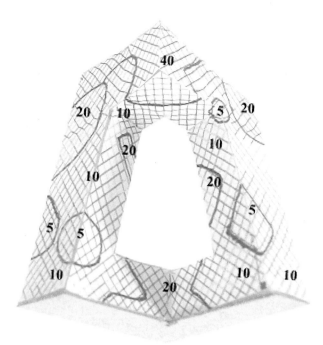

Structural diagram of triangulation density (in meters)
required for uniform stress distribution

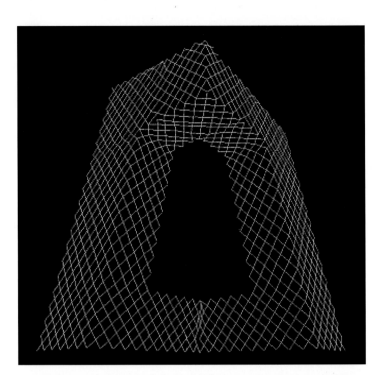

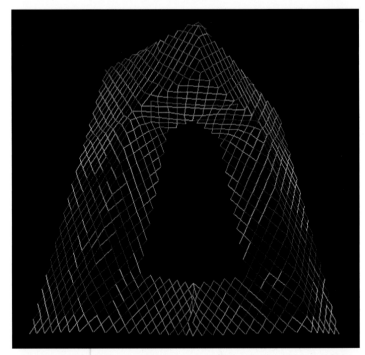

Structural analysis, showing (TOP) uniform diagonals, (CENTER) stress levels on uniform zones, and
(BOTTOM) a redistribution of diagonals accordingly

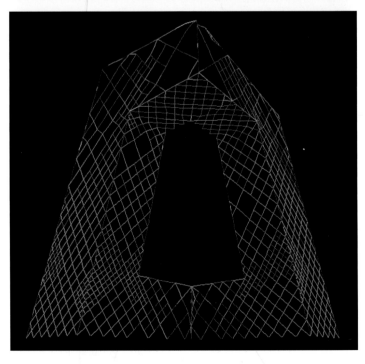

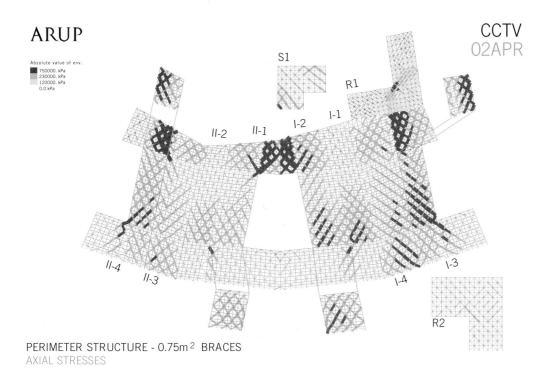

ARUP

Unmodified perimeter structure, axial stress

Absolute value of env.
- 750000. kPa
- 230000. kPa
- 120000. kPa
- 0.0 kPa

S1

R1

II-2 II-1 I-2 I-1

II-4 II-3 I-4 I-3

R2

PERIMETER STRUCTURE - 0.75m² BRACES
AXIAL STRESSES

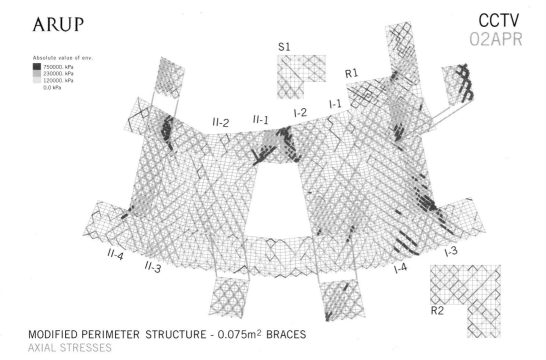

ARUP

Modified perimeter structure, axial stress

Absolute value of env.
- 750000. kPa
- 230000. kPa
- 120000. kPa
- 0.0 kPa

S1

R1

II-2 II-1 I-2 I-1

II-4 II-3 I-4 I-3

R2

MODIFIED PERIMETER STRUCTURE - 0.075m² BRACES
AXIAL STRESSES

BELOW LEFT Sections showing elevator banks
BELOW RIGHT Heating and cooling diagram

768 ft. (234 m)

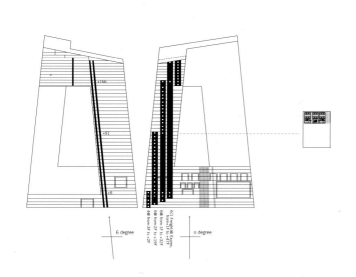

6 degree   0 degree

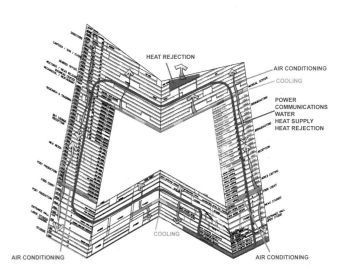

HEAT REJECTION

AIR CONDITIONING
COOLING

POWER
COMMUNICATIONS
WATER
HEAT SUPPLY
HEAT REJECTION

AIR CONDITIONING   COOLING   AIR CONDITIONING

TOP Model
BOTTOM Model detail

View from below (computer-generated image)

768 ft. (234 m)

Highcliff and The Summit

Hong Kong, China
1995–2002

Architect: Dennis Lau Wing-kwong | Dennis Lau & Ng Chun Man
    Architects and Engineers
Engineer: Ad Gouwerok | Magnusson Klemencic Associates

HIGHCLIFF: 827 FEET (252 METERS) HIGH
THE SUMMIT: 722 FEET (220 METERS) HIGH

Highcliff is one of the tallest entirely residential buildings in the world. Its minimal plan of two intersecting ellipses creates a remarkably small footprint but allows generous living spaces above. Such a design, with a focus on maximum density with minimal impact on the landscape, is characteristic of Hong Kong, in which approximately eighty percent of its small territory still remains undeveloped. In the architect Dennis Lau Wing-kwong's words: "The slender Highcliff is very much a creation of the freedom to build high that pertains to Hong Kong." It rises sixty-two stories atop a seven-story sunlit base to a height of 827 feet. Each of its seventy-three, 57-by-157-foot, stories offers two four-bedroom apartments. Service cores are contained within the intersection of the ellipses.

The tower sits on a steep and windy site, one of the windiest in Hong Kong. While the streamlined, curvilinear form somewhat mitigates the effects of the acute wind coming up and over the hillside, the tower had to be skillfully engineered for severe wind forces and typhoons because of its extreme slenderness. Liquid, or sloshing, dampers that control acceleration due to wind forces are located on the roof of the building. They are tuned, according to their length, water depth, and location, to the natural frequency of the building. Waves are induced within the tanks in a phase that opposes the lateral movement of the building, literally slowing it down by acting as massive and dynamic counterweights to oscillations. The podium cuts back and anchors ninety-eight feet into the hillside. The forces of the uphill ground on the base are seven times the total of wind forces. To resist this, a combination of bored piles, a thick mat foundation, basement slabs, and concrete walls form a composite system atop bedrock, which provides a very stiff base. The superstructure's reinforced-concrete core walls, located at the intersection of the ellipses, are joined to a large column on the east facade by a concrete dividing wall. Doorways are vertically aligned and offset on alternating floors to allow the wall to maintain the necessary stiffness. Similar dividing walls are present in each apartment. These and the core walls form building-wide I-beams that provide lateral stiffness in the slender (northeast to southwest) direction. Perimeter floor beams and continuous walls at each of the refuge floors further enhance stiffness.

To the northwest of Highcliff lies the Summit building, a sixty-story apartment building of four-bedroom duplexes, located on Mount Nicholson. The Summit's organic form is similarly slim, particularly at its wings, and subject to wind forces and weather conditions comparable to those of Highcliff. Similar technologies—an excavated base podium, central core, and sloshing dampers at the roof—are implemented to add stiffness.

When viewed from the nearby city, these buildings are unmistakable, forming a distinct pair of slender stems along the hillside skyline. Close-up they have a striking relationship—one concave, one convex—shaping the space between them.
    —Tina di Carlo

Site plan

827 ft. (252 m)

View looking northwest

TOP Highcliff, axonometric of structural computer model
BOTTOM Highcliff, typical floor plan

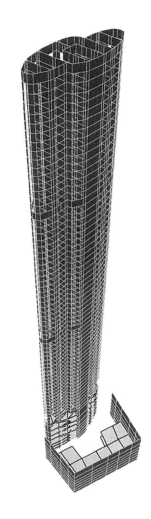

Close-up view of Highcliff

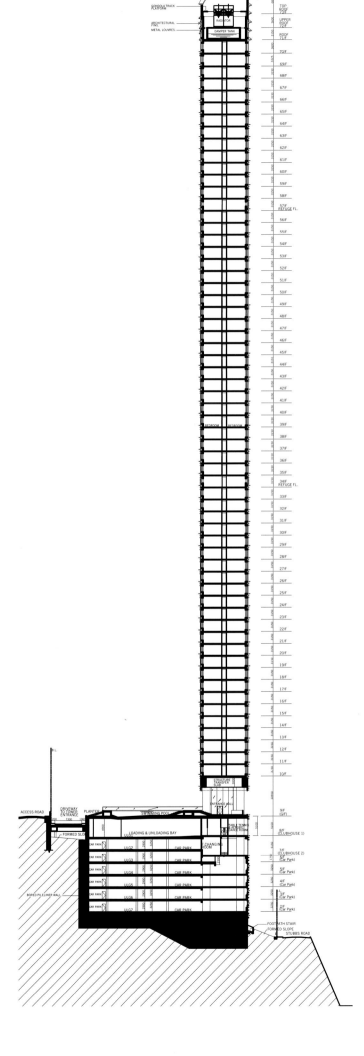

827 ft. (252 m)

Highcliff, transverse section

TOP Construction photograph,
Highcliff and The Summit
BOTTOM The Summit, typical floor plan

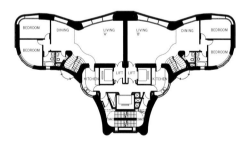

RIGHT View of The Summit looking south

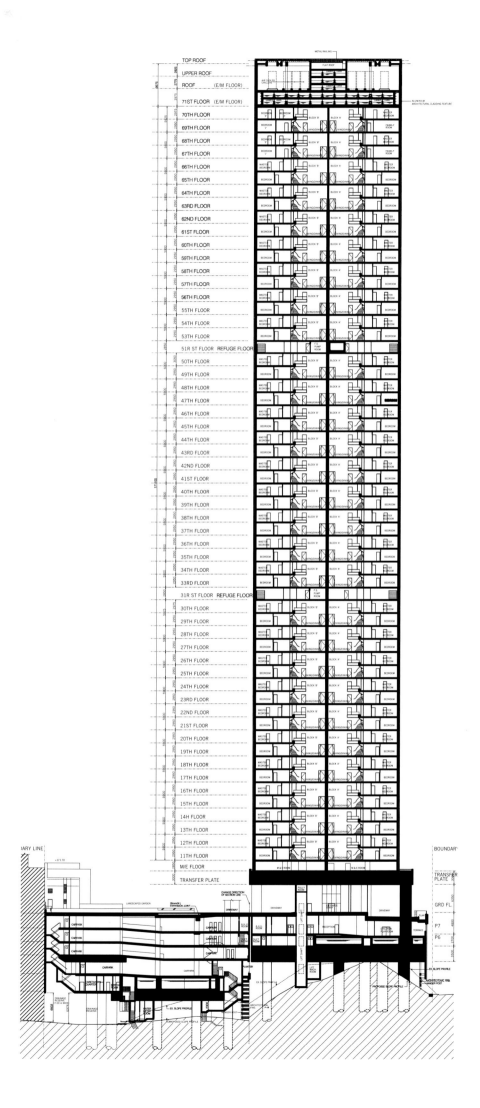

The Summit, longitudinal section

JR Ueno Railway Station Redevelopment

Ueno, Tokyo, Japan
Project, 1988–95

Architect: Arata Isozaki | Arata Isozaki & Associates
Engineer: Toshihiko Kimura | Kimura Structural Engineers

987 FEET (301 METERS) HIGH

The program for the redevelopment of the JR Ueno Railroad Station is typical of the recent Japanese trend for building train stations as mixed-use facilities. Ueno is one of Tokyo's three main railway terminals, and its program called for a hotel of 1,076,000 square feet, a department store of 861,000 square feet, a theater, an art gallery, and interior additions and reconfigurations of the existing station; the total floor area was to be 2.8 million square feet. Although Arata Isozaki's design was altered several times between 1988 and 1995, his interest in creating cultural and physical continuity within the surrounding urban context of Ueno Park and in creating a large multi-use atrium inside the station remained constant.

The overall scheme is configured around three megastructures. One is a quarter-circle structure housing the station's central concourse and department store. The concourse, 79 feet high by 328 feet long, is on the lower level, and a department store surrounds it and occupies the upper level as well. In its upper regions the concourse is pierced by escalators and bridges, which were part of the hotel and department store circulation routes, merging the complex's various programs.

The second structure is an artificial ground plane to the south, above the railway tracks, over which are an oval banquet hall for the hotel, a roof garden, a theater, and a museum. These cultural facilities are intended to augment those of nearby Ueno Park, on the hill directly to the west, thereby extending the cultural zone of many of Tokyo's major museums to the railway station complex.

The third element is a 987-foot-high tower housing mainly hotel suites and offices. In order to avoid blocking sunlight from Ueno Park, the tower needed to be particularly narrow. Its slender footprint and considerable height created a strong whirlwind effect that meant that the tower required extra support. Four enormous buttresses, or struts, were elegantly integrated into the design and unified the three elements of the complex visually. Structurally, the innovative exterior buttresses were studied in detail by computer simulation to determine their response to possible seismic forces and were reviewed by the Japanese National Building Board.

The buttresses, at the first and second tower blocks, support a tower divided into five blocks (six, including the concourse block), each 164 feet high. Each unit is intended to function as an autonomous building, separated from the next by a buffer zone containing mechanical functions. The ingenious design scheme calls for the walls of each of the units to bow outward slightly, a further emphasis of each block's individuality. The curved surfaces also create a series of open corners, which, along with the "quilted" profile, helps reduce the wind load.

—Bevin Cline

987 ft. (301 m)

ABOVE Model
RIGHT Sketch

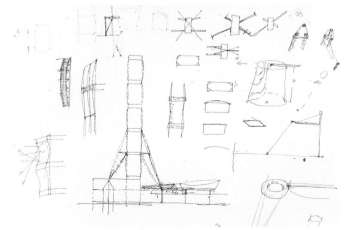

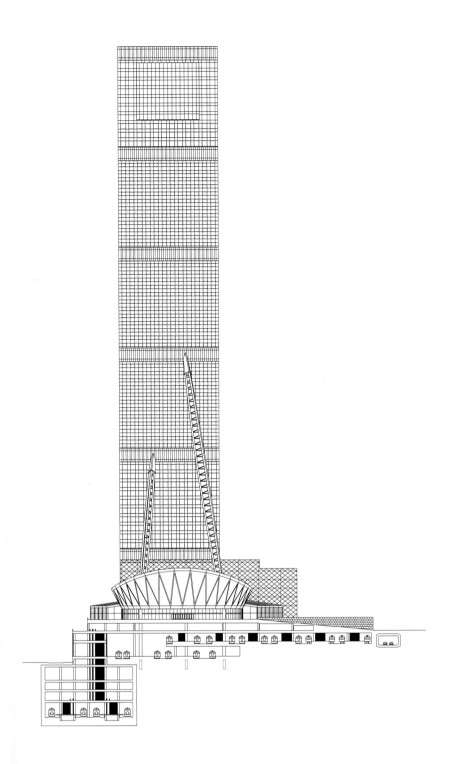

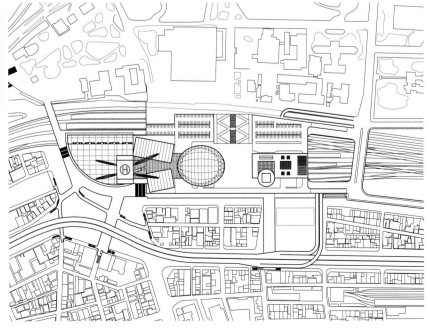

TOP LEFT Elevation
BOTTOM LEFT Site plan
BOTTOM RIGHT Typical floor plan of tower hotel

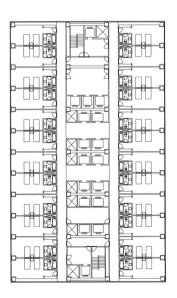

ABOVE Model detail
LEFT Structural diagram

987 ft. (301 m)

5.1 解析モデル

17質点モデル

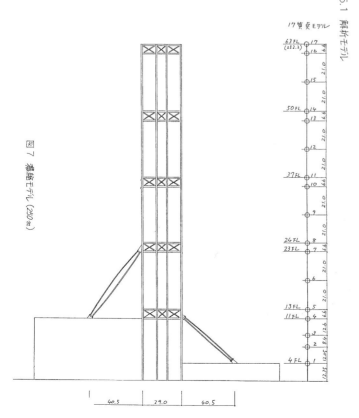

図7 模結モデル (250 m)

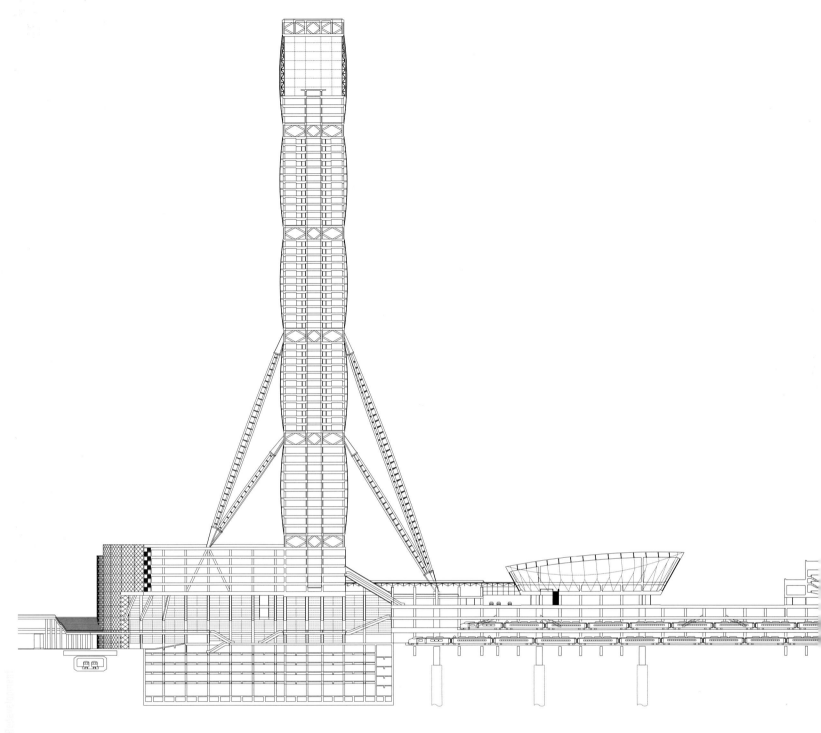

Section, east–west

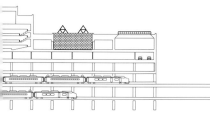

Model detail

987 ft. (301 m)

London Bridge Tower

London, England
Design, 2000—03; projected completion, 2009

Architect: Renzo Piano | Renzo Piano Building Workshop
Engineer: Ove Arup & Partners

1,016 FEET (310 METERS) HIGH

Renzo Piano designed London Bridge Tower as "a sharp and light presence in the skyline." Referring to the spires of London's churches and the masts of the tall ships that used to moor on the Thames River, the tower is generous at the base and slims as it rises into the skyline. Its multisided form responds to the irregularity of the site: each shard of the glass facade forms an inclined plane of what abstractly appears to be a pyramidal form but which is, in fact, a composition of inclined, faceted planes, elegantly proportioned to reach a height of 1,016 feet. Designed with the sight lines of both the occupier and street-level observer in mind, the tower provides a central yet subtle presence on London's low-lying eastern skyline while permitting a panoramic view of the city beyond.

The sixty-six-story tower is to be built on the site of Southwark Towers (a project of the 1970s), adjacent to London Bridge Station. It will be immediately accessible to commuters arriving at this rail station. The Southwark Towers were an effort to redevelop the site of London's first railway line, which was badly damaged during World War II. Piano's redesign proposes to demolish the existing towers and effectively improve the "permeability of the street" by eliminating the series of tracks that divides the area north to south; by adding a large cantilevered, lightweight glass canopy over the plaza; and by lifting it off the ground to pull street level activity—shops, museums, gardens, and restaurants—vertically through the building. The lower levels will be completely open to public programs as well as to office space; the secondary levels, dedicated to hotel apartments; and the third tiers, reserved for residential use. Lobbies given over to public use such as viewing platforms, retail, and winter gar-dens will be positioned at the ground level, mid-section, and upper level, respectively. Winter gardens with operable louver windows will occupy the areas between the shards, permitting contact not only with the outside world but also allowing the building to breathe. "A modern solution to adding density to the city center," the tower will reformulate one of the city's major transportation hubs and maximize public use near the resultant nodes—a key to sustaining the city's future development and regenerating the surrounding neighborhood.

Adhering to Piano's dictum that a modern building must be sustainable from the "human, technological, energetic and economic points of view," the building is economically designed: its tapering form naturally reduces deflection and wind load at the top, and thus places less demand on its central structural concrete core and the mid-level steel outrigger. The floor structure is a carefully integrated system of raised floors, slabs, tapered steel beams, and mechanical ventilation systems. The floor-to-floor height is a very efficient two and a half feet, with a comfortable ceiling height of nine feet. At its completion in 2009 the building will consume thirty percent less energy than a standard building of its size. Apartments and hotel rooms are heated with the excess heat from the offices; and that excess heat will be dissipated and cooled through a dry-air cooler at the top of the tower. The double-ventilated facade will reduce solar gain and, in turn, reduce air-conditioning requirements and improve thermal comfort close to the windows. All glass will be untinted and extra white to enhance the building's sense of a light, crystalline, open form.

—Tina di Carlo

BELOW Sketch
OPPOSITE View from the street
(computer-generated image)

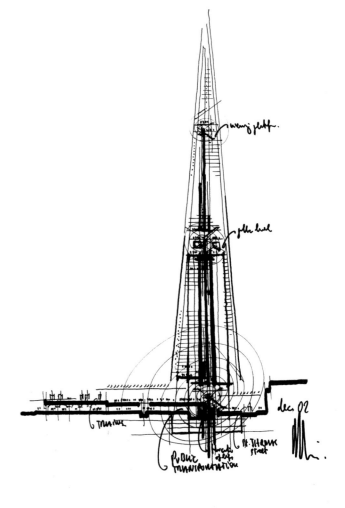

1,016 ft. (310 m)

View looking southeast across the Thames River

Site plan and ground-floor plan

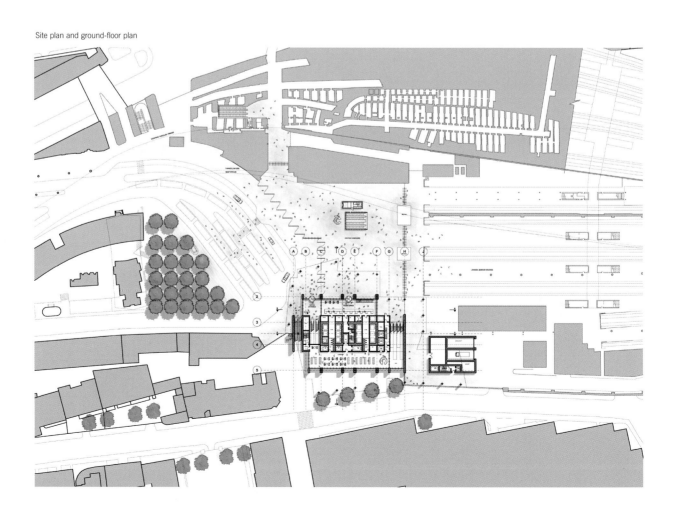

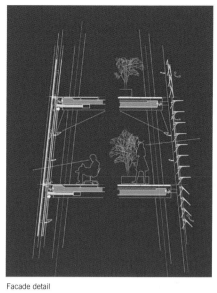

Facade detail

Typical upper-level floor plan

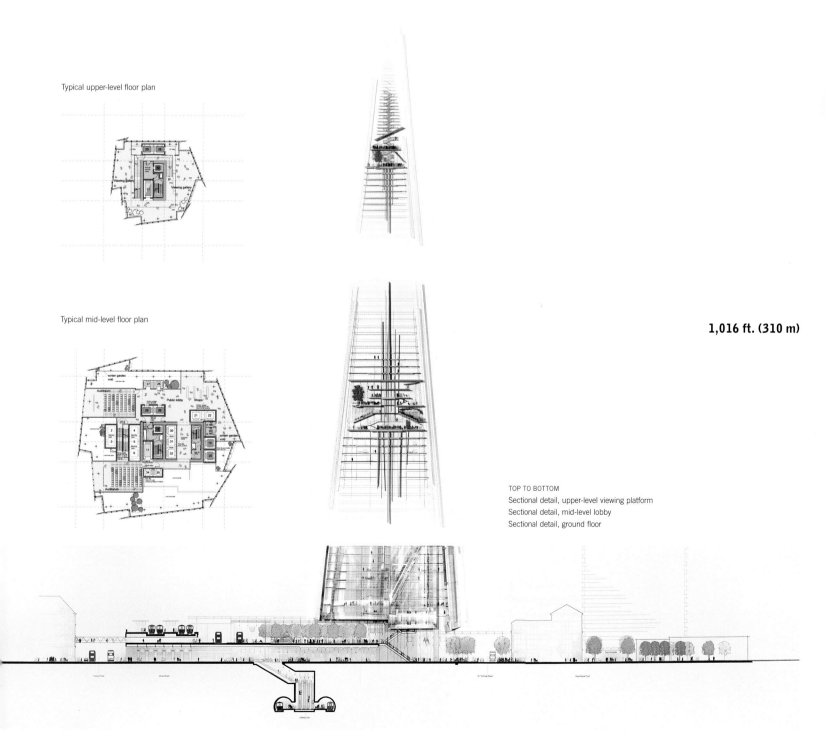

Typical mid-level floor plan

1,016 ft. (310 m)

TOP TO BOTTOM
Sectional detail, upper-level viewing platform
Sectional detail, mid-level lobby
Sectional detail, ground floor

World Trade Center

New York, New York
Project, 2002

**Architects: Richard Meier | Richard Meier & Partners Architects;
Peter Eisenman | Eisenman Architects; Charles Gwathmey |
Gwathmey Siegel & Associates; Stephen Holl | Steven Holl Architects
Engineer: Craig Schwitters | Buro Happold**

1,111 FEET (337 METERS) HIGH

Designed as part of the competition for a master plan for the site of the former World Trade Center towers, this proposal consists of two narrow slab-like towers, rather than conventional towers, one running east–west along Vesey Street and the other running north–south along Church Street. The project-specific team of designers (Peter Eisenman, Charles Gwathmey, Steven Holl, and Richard Meier) describes each of these two structures as a "matrix of voids and solids" reaching 1,111 feet tall with a total area of 8.5 million square feet.

The building on Vesey Street consists of two vertical and four horizontal elements, and that on Church Street has three vertical elements. The cantilevered ends of the two structures reach toward each other but don't touch, visually knitting the two towers together without physically connecting them.

High-strength concrete shear walls form the vertical interior cores. These walls are oriented in the long direction to reduce the amount of structure in the facades and maximize sunlight and views. The shear walls are also situated so as to provide the cores with maximum protection, and columns are specified as high-strength composite concrete and steel.

Steel bridges link the vertical cores creating "super floors" of approximately 80,000 square feet in the Vesey Street tower and 110,000 square feet in the Church Street tower. Stability in the short direction is achieved by bracing frames in the cores in the lateral direction.

The relatively small footprint of the towers insures a lightness and permeability that is the opposite of the squat "fireplug" profile of recent speculative office towers with maximized area. Still, smaller floor plates require the same amount of elevator stops and more innovation in the traffic design. In this instance, the designers have specified three elevator zones and two sky lobbies. A double-decker express elevator ferries passengers to the sky lobbies from which local elevator service continues to all floors.

The innovative formal conception of the towers—a powerful abstraction on the New York skyline—presents equally inventive modes of occupancy. A tenant could occupy a typical horizontal floor plate or lease spaces that are arranged vertically, or staggered, or even looped around one of the voids. Additionally, the super-floor linkages between cores would allow for multiple routes of escape and fire fighter access along a combination of vertical and horizontal paths.

To reduce the solar-heat gain, the south and west facades have double-glazing with an air gap to exhaust heat before it enters the building envelope. The air gap is illuminated at night via power stored in photovoltaic cells. The "glow" of the building at night reflects the intensity of the day's solar activity. Solar panels on the roof provide auxiliary electricity.

In addition to literally framing public space at ground level, the gridded towers seek to maintain a public presence within as well. Public space exists at the top in the form of observation decks, conference centers, restaurants, a hotel, and a memorial chapel, insuring that high-rises in New York maintain the dream of the vertical city.

—Terence Riley

View looking east across the Hudson River
(computer-generated image)

Perspective, by Steven Holl

1,111 ft. (337 m)

Conceptual sketches, by Peter Eisenman

Conceptual sketches, by Richard Meier

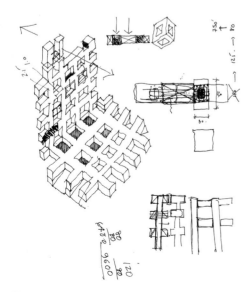

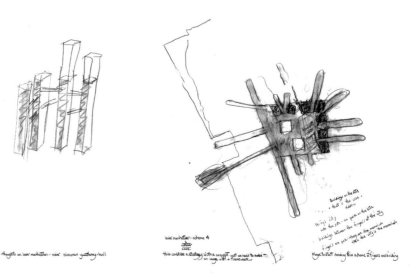

TOP LEFT Perspective of entry, by Steven Holl
BOTTOM LEFT Typical floor plans

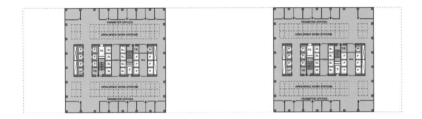

Section of site, north–south

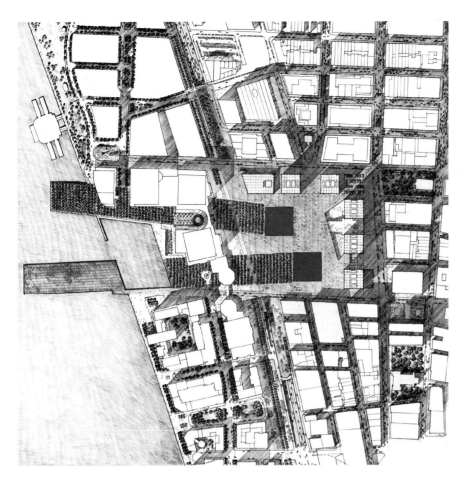

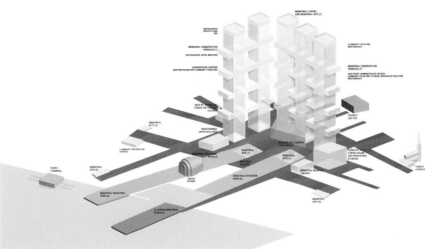

1,111 ft. (337 m)

TOP Site plan, by Laurie Olin
BOTTOM Axonometric, showing programmatic
distribution (computer-generated image)
RIGHT View looking south from street at night

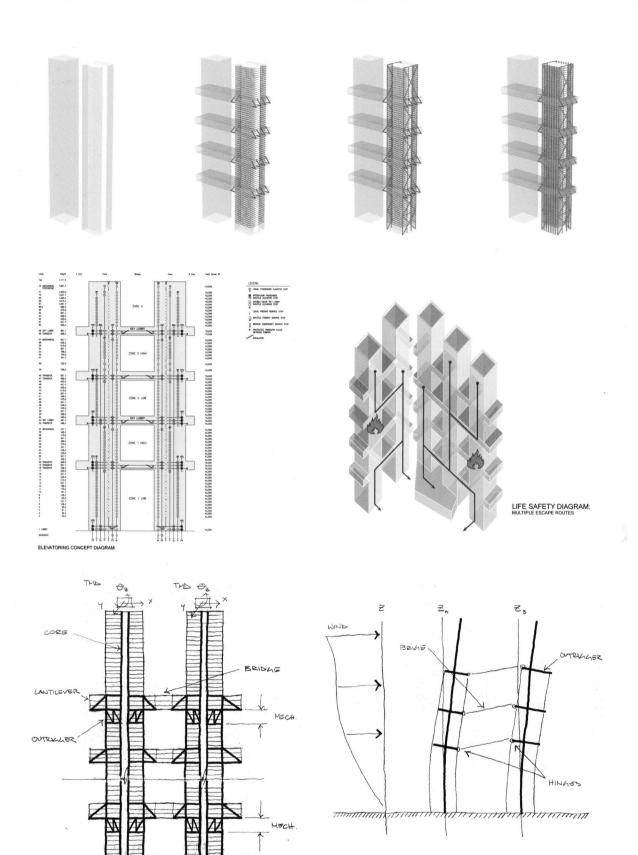

TOP Diagram of trussing system
CENTER LEFT Elevator diagram
CENTER RIGHT Life-safety diagram
BOTTOM LEFT Diagram of outrigger structure
BOTTOM RIGHT Wind-deflection diagram

Model, showing park to the Hudson River

1,111 ft. (337 m)

View looking southeast from the Hudson River
(computer-generated image)

131

New York Times Headquarters

New York, New York
Design, 2000—03; projected completion, 2006

Architect: Renzo Piano | Renzo Piano Building Workshop
Engineer: Thomas Scarangello | Thornton-Tomasetti Engineers

1,140 FEET (348 METERS) HIGH

In 2000, Renzo Piano's competition entry for the New York Times Headquarters was selected as the winning scheme, and is presently under construction near Times Square in Manhattan.

The shape of the slender tower is straightforward, a simple rectangle reflecting Manhattan's grid. The architectural and structural metaphor derives from the newspaper's own values: clarity and transparency. The tower is sheathed in a double-layered envelope: a glass curtain wall enclosing the structure and a screen of clear glass and ceramic rods suspended one to two feet in front of it. The screen wall both deflects solar gain and heightens atmospheric effect.

At ground level, the building is open and permeable. Restraurants and a semipublic auditorium ring an internal garden. A passage allows the public into the garden area and connects Fortieth and Forty-first streets. Just above the street, the New York Times newsroom occupies three levels, visible from the street and continuously active. According to the architect, this arrangement reflects the fact that "it is from the street itself that the newspaper metaphorically gathers its inspiration."

The transparent skin of the building not only echoes the organization of the newspaper within, it also reveals an elegant structural solution. On Eighth Avenue, the tripartite main facade is clearly expressed in the central shaft of the tower and lateral wings. An internal Vierendeel truss supports the central portion, from which exposed tension rods support the southernmost and northernmost twenty feet of the structure. Lateral stability is achieved through a sixty-five-by-ninety-foot braced core. In the four corners of the tower, the exterior X-braced frames bracketing the tower are visible. Their vertical ascent, mirrored in the placement of the intercommunicating stairs, is also visible from the side streets.

While the lower portions of the tower reflect the hustle and bustle of the street and the omnipresence of the media, the roof offers a more contemplative environment, protected by screen walls of glass and ceramic rods. A four-hundred-foot mast rises above a roof garden framed by spaces for meetings. Backlit by the changing position of the sun, the diaphanous crown of the tower will assume its own identity within Manhattan's high-rise skyline.

—Terence Riley

Sketch

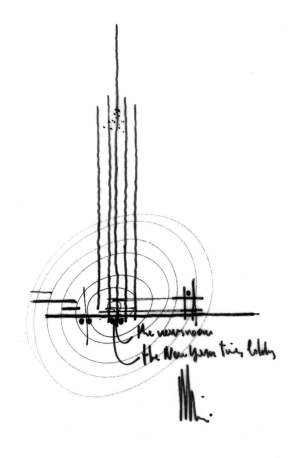

1,140 ft. (348 m)

Model

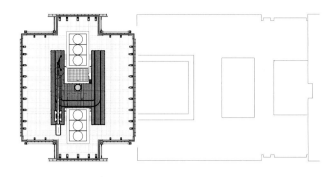

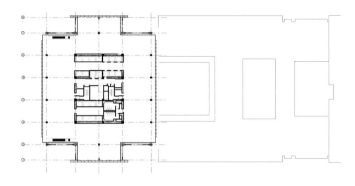

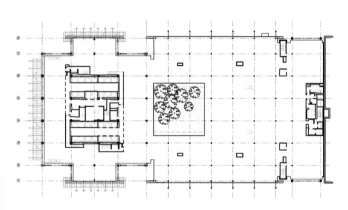

TOP TO BOTTOM
Plan, rooftop tower
Typical floor plan, upper levels
Plan of newsroom, floor 2

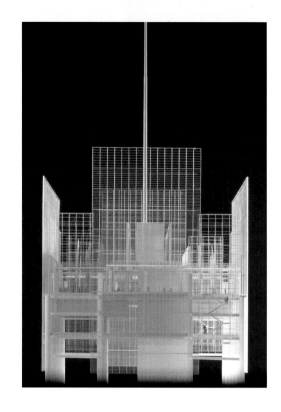

TOP TO BOTTOM
Model of rooftop detail
Model, showing height relative to the Chrysler
Building and the Empire State Building
Site plan

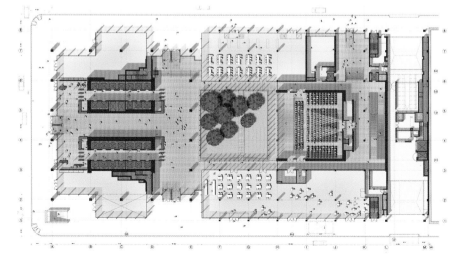

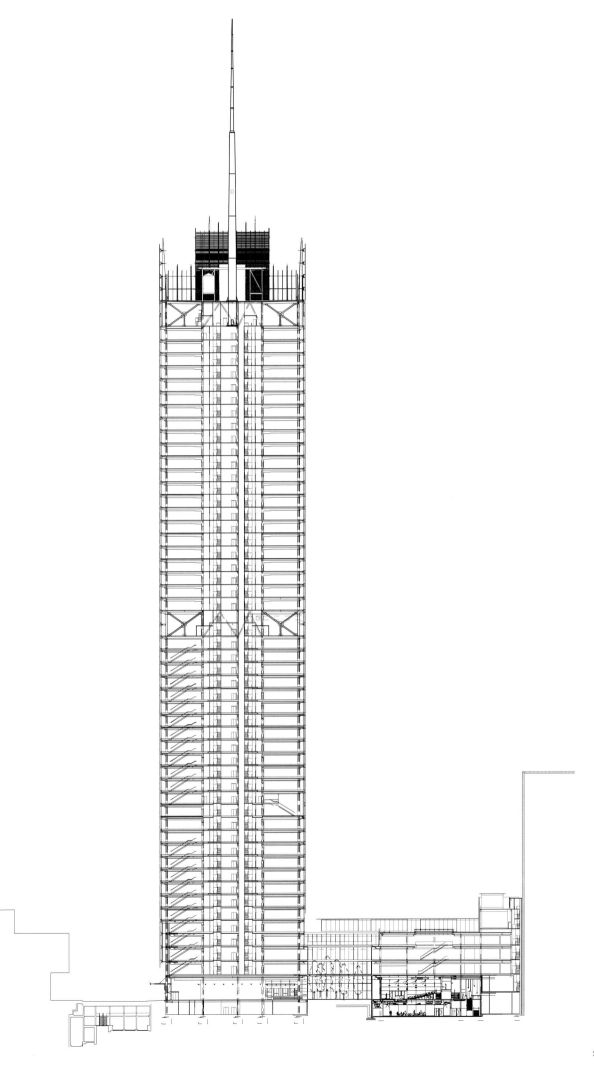

1,140 ft. (348 m)

Section

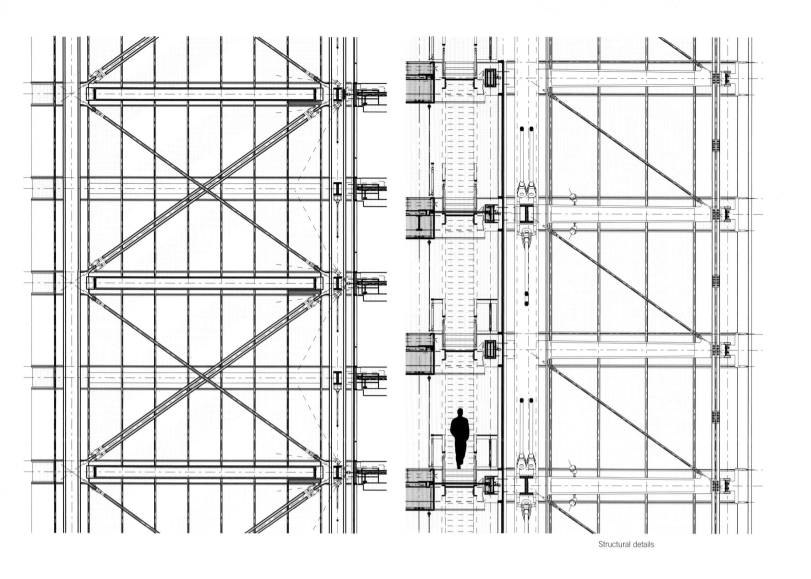

Structural details

Facade detail

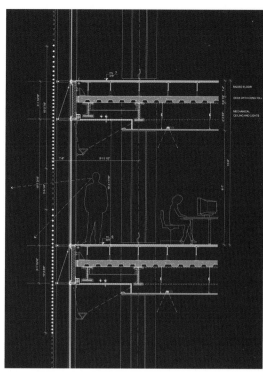

Structural detail

1,140 ft. (348 m)

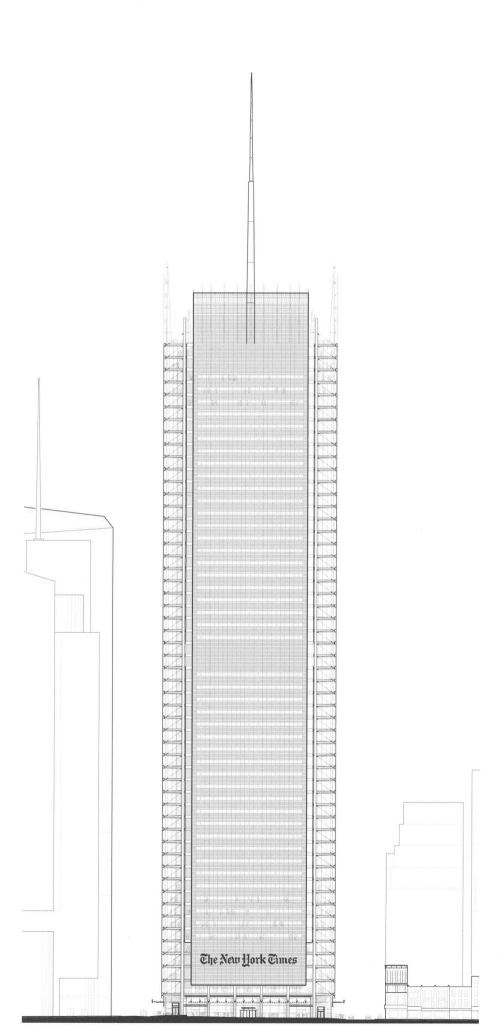

East elevation

Jin Mao Tower

Pudong New Area, Shanghai, China
1993–99

Architect: Adrian D. Smith | Skidmore, Owings & Merrill
Engineer: D. Stanton Korista | Skidmore, Owings & Merrill

1,380 FEET (421 METERS) HIGH

Adrian D. Smith and D. Stanton Korista designed the decorative and opulent Jin Mao Tower to create a unique presence on the Shanghai skyline that recalls the ancient form of the Chinese pagoda. The tower is located in the Pudong New Area, a large plot of farmland reclaimed in the early 1990s to foster China's modernization and emergence into the global financial market. The ancient pagoda, a form indigenous to China, was one of the world's first tall buildings. Historically, it symbolizes the village gathering place and seemed a fitting choice for a building meant to be the new center of Shanghai.

The Jin Mao is an eighty-eight-story mixed-use tower, constituting part of an eight-million-square-foot development. It was the world's fourth tallest building in 1999 when it was completed and is still the tallest in China. The lower fifty stories are dedicated to office space; the upper thirty-eight floors provide a 555-room hotel. The podium at the base houses a conference and exhibition center, an auditorium, and 226,000 square feet of retail space.

The tower telescopes upward in progressive, rhythmic increments based on a proportion of the number eight. The increments decrease gradually to create an eight-sided crenellated apex and crown, described by the architect as "a culmination of the stepping system clustered and transformed into a profile and surface composition that can be identified from several kilometers away." Granite, stainless steel, aluminum, and glass comprise the silver facade. These materials create a luminous effect in harmony with the sky and the changing light reflected from the Yangtze River. The vertical mullions are spaced consistently at twenty-nine inches, and large stainless-steel sun-shading grills are set at about floor level, together forming a surface density that mediates between the scale of the tower and that of the street.

In plan, the Jin Mao maintains a bi-axial symmetry, a device characteristic of the pagoda but also one that responds to a 360-degree view. The plan is cruciform, marked by an octagonal structural core. The interior of the core is dedicated to services for the lower fifty stories and to the tower's central feature, the hotel atrium, in the upper thirty-eight. What is essentially a dark space of services and structure at the bottom is turned inside out to become a light-filled atrium, with its sublime and vertiginous scale, seemingly almost hyper-real in its repetition. The spiraling, gold balconies overlooking the hotel lobby exacerbate this effect. A glass arch on the atrium's northeast side contains six elevators that service the hotel.

The structure is a kind of stayed mast. The central core of reinforced-concrete walls is linked at three levels—between floors twenty-six and twenty-eight, fifty-one and fifty-three, and eighty-five and eighty-seven—by two-story-high outrigger trusses to eight main exterior super-frame columns. These act as stays to stiffen the core mast. To allow for relative movement due to creep, shrinkage, elastic shortening, and temperature during construction, the outrigger truss connections between the structural core and exterior composite mega-columns employ large-diameter structural-steel pins in circular and slotted holes.

The foundation was designed to withstand typhoon winds reaching up to 125 miles per hour, earthquakes, and generally poor soil conditions. Open-end structural-steel piles capped with a thirteen-foot-thick reinforced-concrete mat extend 270 feet into the ground. A three-foot-thick, 118-foot-deep slurry wall acts as a temporary retaining wall, a permanent water cut-off wall, and a permanent foundation wall. Such a structural configuration was chosen, according to the architect and engineer, for its optimum stiffness against the high winds of Shanghai, speed of construction, and efficient use of materials. The wide column spacing at the perimeter avoids any interior columns, thus providing maximum interior flexibility, light, and uninterrupted views.

The axis of the ancient pagoda structure consisted of a large pillar that floated above the ground, held by the upward force of all the cantilever rafters—a kind of floating mast. The Jin Mao Tower cleverly reverses this with a firmly nested mast and a dramatic void suspended above. The building is a landmark in Shanghai and a pioneer in the creation of complex skyscraper spaces.
—Tina di Carlo

BELOW Sketches
OPPOSITE View looking across the Yangtze River toward the Pudong New District

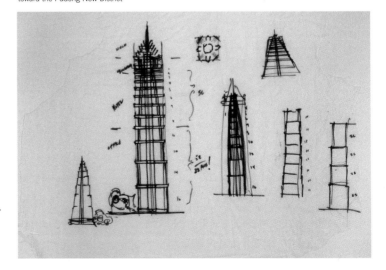

1,380 ft. (421 m)

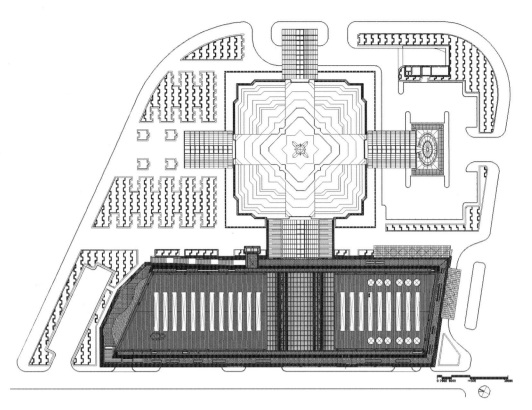

Roof plan and site plan

View of hotel atrium, looking
down toward hotel lobby

TOP TO BOTTOM
Typical floor plan, upper levels
Typical floor plan, hotel and atrium
Ground-floor plan

RIGHT Section

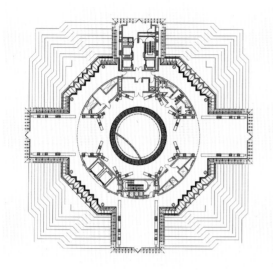

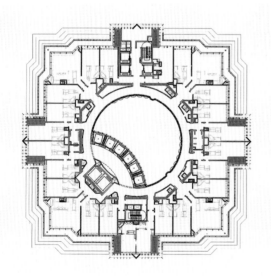

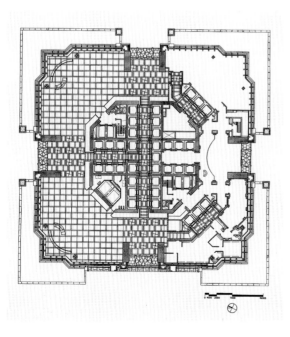

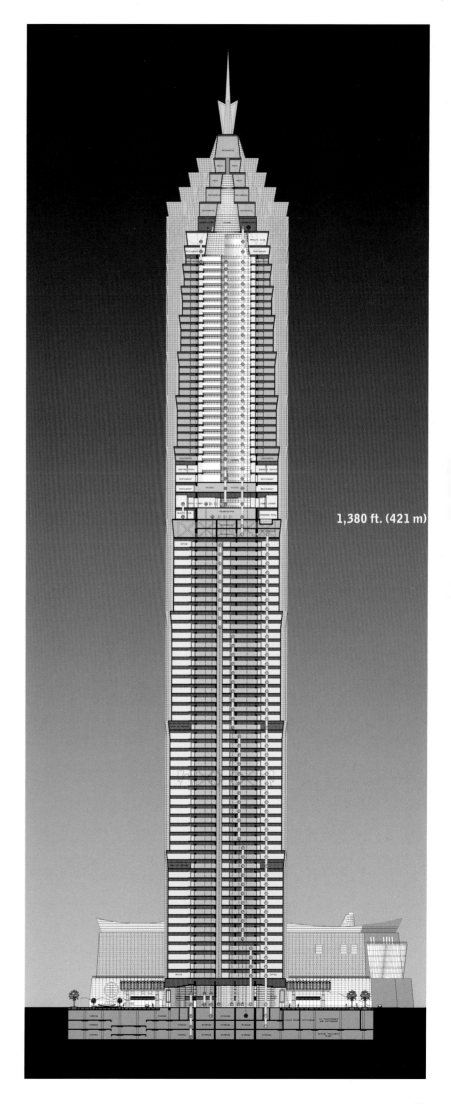

1,380 ft. (421 m)

View of crown

TOP View from below
BOTTOM Facade detail
RIGHT Southwest facade

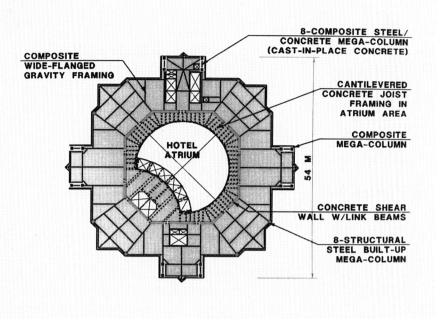

Hotel framing plan

COMPOSITE WIDE-FLANGED GRAVITY FRAMING

8-COMPOSITE STEEL/ CONCRETE MEGA-COLUMN (CAST-IN-PLACE CONCRETE)

CANTILEVERED CONCRETE JOIST FRAMING IN ATRIUM AREA

COMPOSITE MEGA-COLUMN

HOTEL ATRIUM

54 M

CONCRETE SHEAR WALL W/LINK BEAMS

8-STRUCTURAL STEEL BUILT-UP MEGA-COLUMN

1,380 ft. (421 m)

Construction photographs

Togok (XL Towers)

Seoul, Korea
Project, 1996–2002

Architect: Rem Koolhaas | Office for Metropolitan Architecture
Engineers: Cecil Balmond, Philip Dilley | Ove Arup & Partners

1,444 FEET (440 METERS) HIGH

Togok (XL Towers) re-invents the typology of the tall building, traditionally defined by the invention of the elevator, steel construction, and electricity. A proposal designed by Rem Koolhaas for a mostly vacant site at the perimeter of Seoul, Korea, Togok consists of a cluster of six buildings of various heights located on a central, elevated plinth. Two of the six towers are arranged and inclined to form A-frames with their opposite towers. The inclined towers link up with the structures opposite them and pass tangentially to the central structure. All are tied together with a structural and circulation collar. While, separately, the buildings would be slender enough to require extensive dynamic control, together they create a stiff ensemble capable of sustaining large lateral, as well as vertical, loads. This connection is further made use of by introducing springs and dampers at the "passing" connections of the inclined central tower to control wind vibrations. This system eschews the need for extremely deep floor plates and a central core that traditionally provides lateral stability. The result is a high degree of spaces with natural daylight and views.

That the structure depends on the combined action of the buildings is paradigmatic of the complex as a whole.

Unlike the solitary skyscraper where most activity occurs inside, Togok is intended create "continuity, variety and programmatic richness," adding to the intensification of urban life. In the words of the architect: "The different elements support each other in every sense: architecturally, they form an integrated complex; technically, issues of stability access, circulation and servicing are organized collectively; urbanistically, the entire building becomes an urban quarter of a new kind."

The complex offers approximately four million square feet of retail space, 1.5 million square feet of hotel accommodations as well as a winter garden, a convention center, restaurants, shops, a fusion hall, a pool, a 10,000-seat stadium, a virtual entertainment center, and extensive underground parking. Main vertical access is provided through two service cores in the central tower. The entire complex connects to the center of the city by subway, bus, tram, and a proposed new monorail system.

True to his 1978 manifesto *Delirious New York*, Koolhaas here proposes an architecture that creates conditions and fabricates content, framing and writing the script of urban life through tectonic means.

—Tina di Carlo

BELOW Sketch
OPPOSITE Model detail

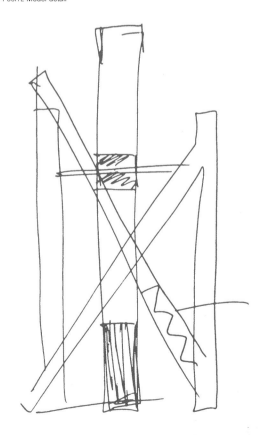

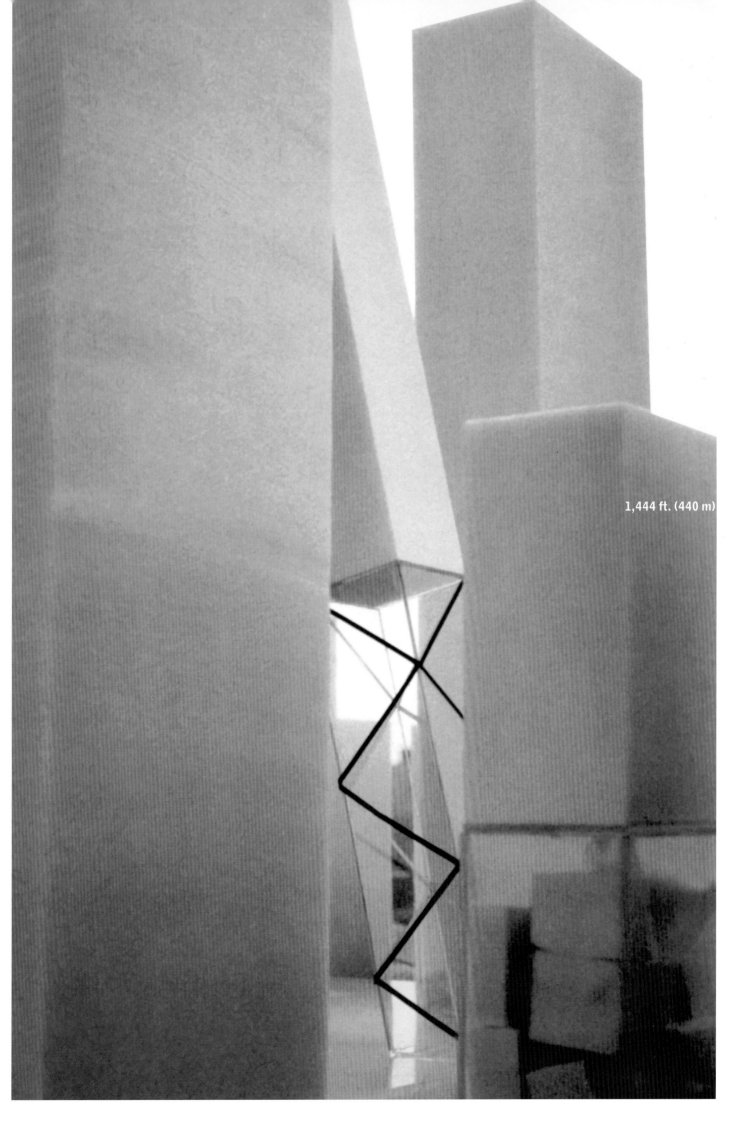

1,444 ft. (440 m)

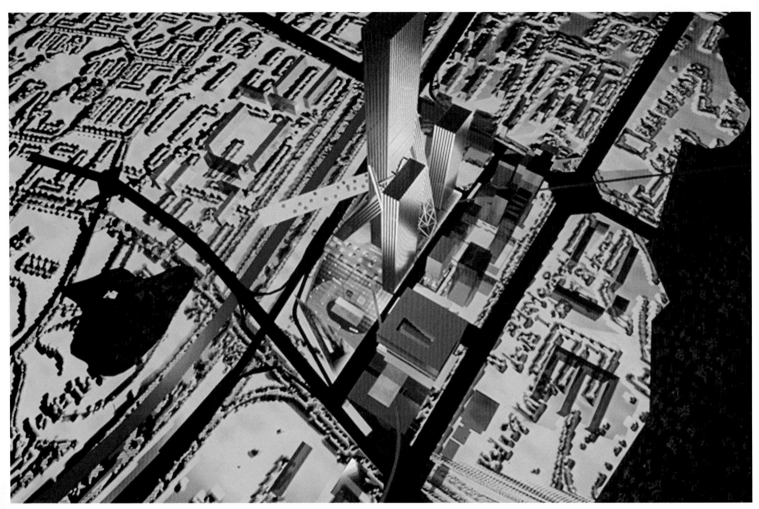

Axonometric and aerial view of site
(computer-generated image)

BELOW AND OPPOSITE Sections

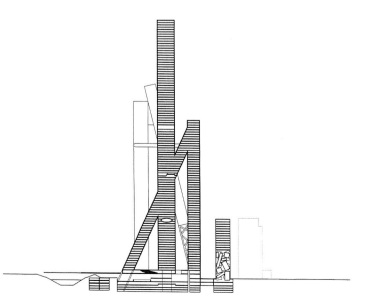

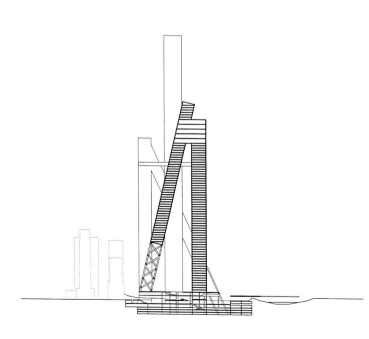

1,444 ft. (440 m)

Elevation

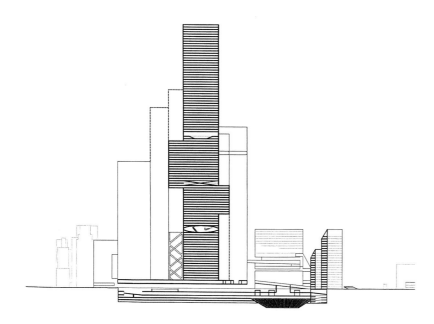

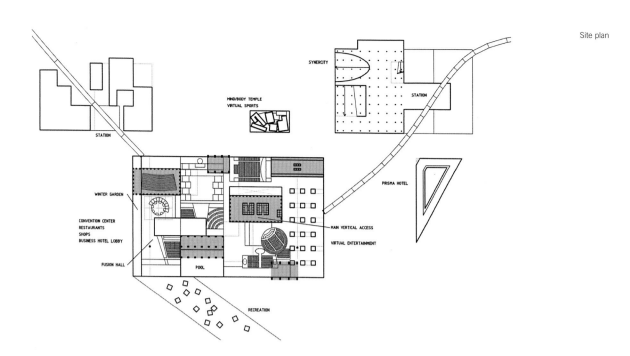

Site plan

STATION

WINTER GARDEN

CONVENTION CENTER
RESTAURANTS
SHOPS
BUSINESS HOTEL LOBBY

FUSION HALL

POOL

RECREATION

MIND/BODY TEMPLE
VIRTUAL SPORTS

MAIN VERTICAL ACCESS

VIRTUAL ENTERTAINMENT

SYNERCITY

STATION

PRISMA HOTEL

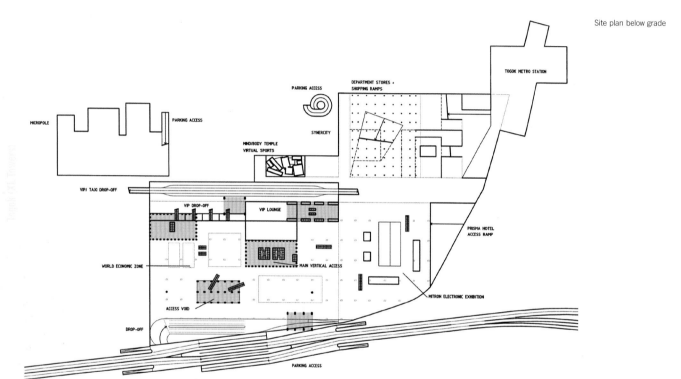

Site plan below grade

MICROPOLE

PARKING ACCESS

PARKING ACCESS

SYNERCITY

MIND/BODY TEMPLE
VIRTUAL SPORTS

DEPARTMENT STORES +
SHOPPING RAMPS

TOGOK METRO STATION

VIP/ TAXI DROP-OFF

VIP DROP-OFF

VIP LOUNGE

WORLD ECONOMIC ZONE

MAIN VERTICAL ACCESS

PRISMA HOTEL
ACCESS RAMP

MITRON ELECTRONIC EXHIBITION

ACCESS VOID

DROP-OFF

PARKING ACCESS

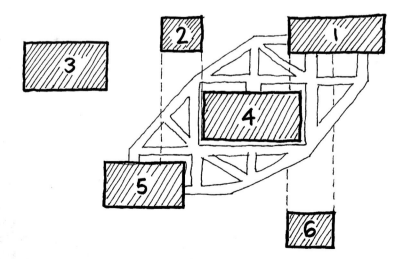

Plan diagram showing collar

1,444 ft. (440 m)

View from above (computer-generated image)

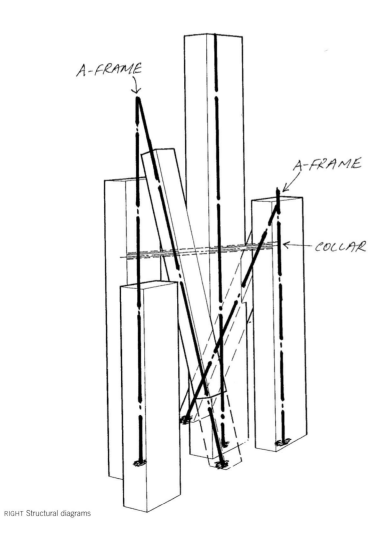

A-FRAME

A-FRAME

COLLAR

RIGHT Structural diagrams

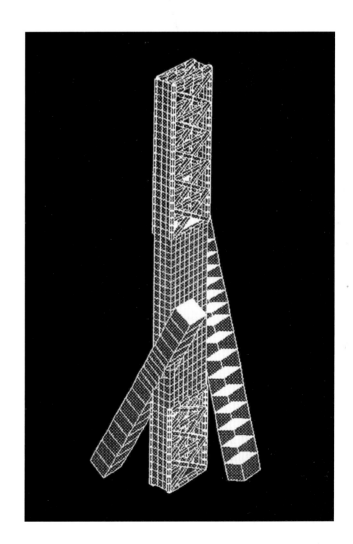

Kowloon Station Tower

Kowloon, Hong Kong, China
Design, 2000—03; projected completion, 2007

Architect: William Pedersen | Kohn Pedersen Fox Associates
Engineers: George Chan | Ove Arup & Partners; Leslie Robertson | LERA

1,583 FEET (475 METERS) HIGH

The 108-story Kowloon Station Tower is one of two very tall structures being built over new transit hubs in Kowloon and Hong Kong Island. They were planned as a result of the construction of the new Chep Lap Kok Airport in Hong Kong, built in 1998. Rapid transit from either hub provides a direct line to the new airport in thirty minutes. The Kowloon tower includes 2.7 million square feet of office space, a 300-room hotel at the top, an observation deck on the ninetieth floor, and retail and parking spaces at ground level over the station platforms.

The building is square in plan, 167 feet on a side, and turned at an angle to the street grid. This turn results from the presence of a deep trench in the soil profile beneath its corners. The turn also distinguishes this important landmark alongside Victoria Harbor. The facade is separated from the rest of the building in four distinct vertical faces that curve into the building at the top forty stories and away from it at the bottom twenty-seven. The corners of the building are notched in plan approximately sixteen feet to create this reveal. The appearance of the curtain wall is further lightened by an unusual shingling design where each row of floor-high panels of glass and metal is tilted 5.25 degrees back at the top. This in-creases the effective interior space for the occupants while limiting the unnecessary cavity space. The floor-to-floor height is thirteen and one-half feet with a shallow raised floor for electrical distribution and a four-foot-high sandwich of ceiling, mechanical distribution, and floor structure.

The vertical structure of the tower is made of a 300-square-foot concrete core with up to five-foot-thick walls of high-strength concrete linked at four levels by steel outrigger trusses tied to eight large concrete columns. The structural design is identical to that of the Hong Kong Island tower across the harbor. Arup's studies of alternative structural systems have indicated that this "mast and outrigger" scheme is costlier than a perimeter tube or braced frame; but the advantages of barrier-free views on all sides afforded by the open centers and minimal number of columns outweigh that additional cost. The outrigger levels correspond to the locations of the refuge floors mandated by Asian tall-building regulations for fire safety, and are distinguished by rectangular panels on the facades. The Kowloon Station Tower is a landmark in the most direct sense and a well-textured synthesis of form and structure.

—Guy Nordenson

BELOW Model detail
OPPOSITE Model

1,583 ft. (475 m)

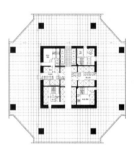

Typical floor plans, upper, middle, and lower levels

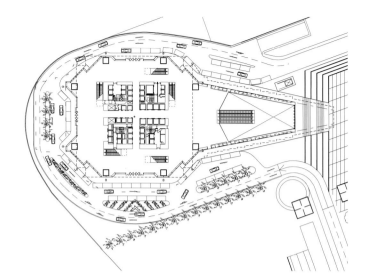

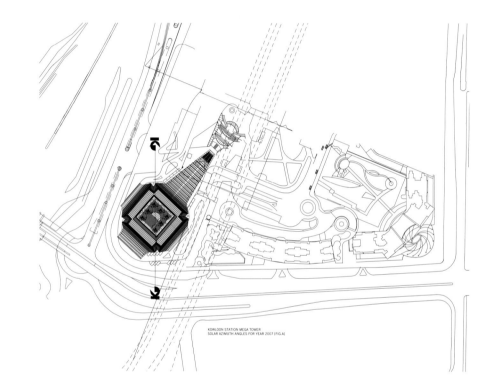

KOWLOON STATION MEGA TOWER
SOLAR AZIMUTH ANGLES FOR YEAR 2007 (FIG.A)

TOP Ground-floor plan
CENTER Site plan
BOTTOM Study of foundation structure

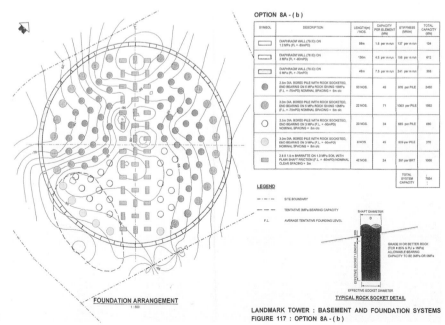

FOUNDATION ARRANGEMENT
1 : 500

LEGEND

--- · --- SITE BOUNDARY

--- --- TENTATIVE 3MPa BEARING CAPACITY

F.L. AVERAGE TENTATIVE FOUNDING LEVEL

TYPICAL ROCK SOCKET DETAIL

LANDMARK TOWER : BASEMENT AND FOUNDATION SYSTEMS
FIGURE 117 : OPTION 8A - (b)

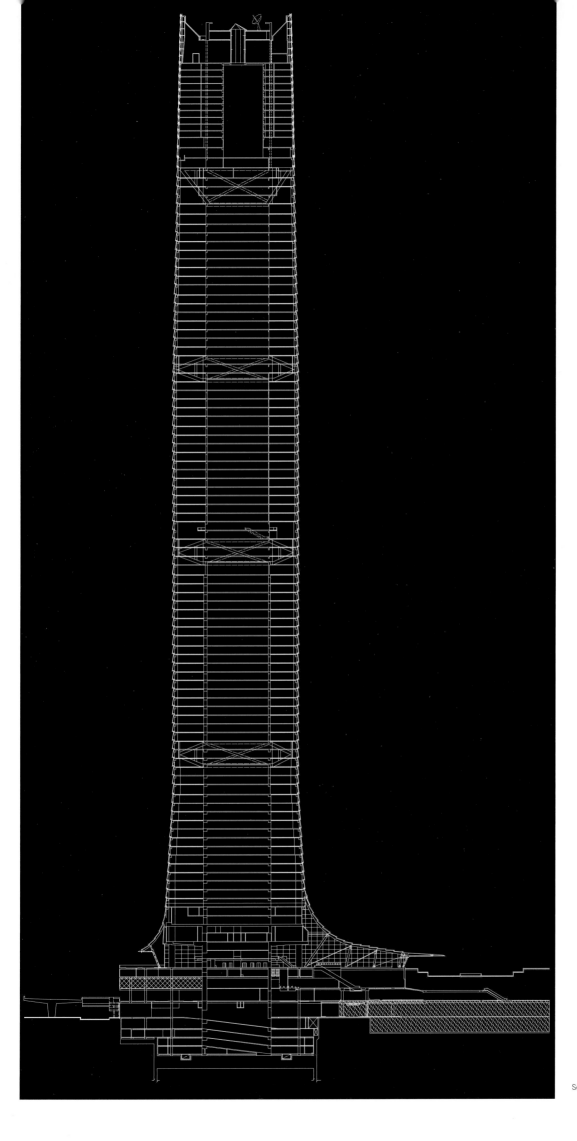

1,583 ft. (475 m)

Section

Model, detail of entry canopy

Detail model, showing interior of entry canopy

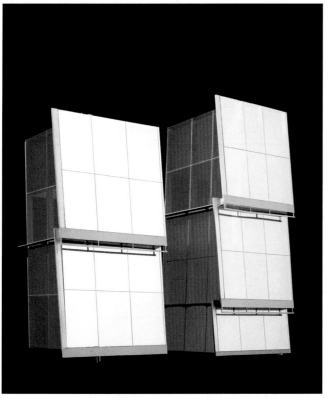

Facade detail

Facade detail, section

1,583 ft. (475 m)

Rooftop detail

World Trade Center

New York, New York
Project, 2002

Architects: United Architects: Ben van Berkel, Caroline Bos | Un Studio;
Peter Frankfurt, Mikon van Gastel | Imaginary Forces; Kevin Kennon |
Kevin Kennon Architects; Greg Lynn | Greg Lynn FORM; Farshid Moussavi,
Alejandro Zaero-Polo | Foreign Office Architects; Jesse Reiser, Nanako
Umemoto | Reiser + Umemoto
Engineers: Aine M. Brazil, Thomas Scarangello | Thornton-Tomasetti;
Rory McGowan | Ove Arup & Partners

1,620 FEET (494 METERS) HIGH

Designed as part of the competition for a master plan for the site of the former World Trade Center towers, the scheme proposed by a project-specific team called United Architects, whose members have offices in the United States and abroad, is actually five linked towers containing over ten million square feet of space. More than eighty percent of the area is designated for office space; the balance is residential, commercial, and cultural. The towers rise over a proposed memorial at ground level as well as an elaborate transportation and retail complex below grade. The ambition of this team in designing the project is clear: "The structural concept for the towers has been developed with the intention of establishing a new tower typology."

The principal elements of each tower are a twenty-foot-square concrete core and two or more volumes of habitable space, which wrap around the core. The supporting framework for the volumes of space is a diagonally braced exterior skin, which, in effect, makes the spaces structural "tubes within tubes" without intervening columns. The geometric flexibility and strength of the triangulated structural skin allows the exterior tubes to expand and contract as they wrap around the core, producing the dynamic appearance of the ensemble.

Each of the five towers is designed as a self-supporting freestanding structure. When they are conjoined, their individual structural strength is increased, making them able to resist tremendous forces through mutual support. In the wake of the September 11 disaster and the public's concerns about the safety of tall buildings, the added strength is an important feature, but is not the only design element created by the bundling of the towers. The conjoined towers, unlike the traditional vertical tower with its unitary vertical systems, offer multiple routes of escape and fire-fighting access following vertical and, if necessary, horizontal routes. This redundancy of circulation can also be found in other systems in the building. For example, the network of sprinkler heads can have multiple sources of water pressure, and in the event of the failure of one another can compensate.

The designers have also tried to restore a sense of safety as well as a sense of wonder in tall buildings. A "sky park" at the top of the complex, with public amenities, creates a lofty horizon at the fifty-fifth floor. The sky park links all of the towers and brings public access and social space to the highest common point of the five structures. At floor 108, the apex of the tallest structure, is an observatory. "Sky gardens" on the roofs of the towers provide further social amenity as well as positive environmental effects.

The connections between the towers create a remarkable silhouette across the skyline, a symbol of collectivity; their gaps also create monumental urban spaces that frame views and channel circulation. Together, the ensemble inspires wonder at its soaring height; but the towers also arc in such a way as to create public space beneath them. The project celebrates the tall building as a technical and cultural artifact.
—Terence Riley

Study model

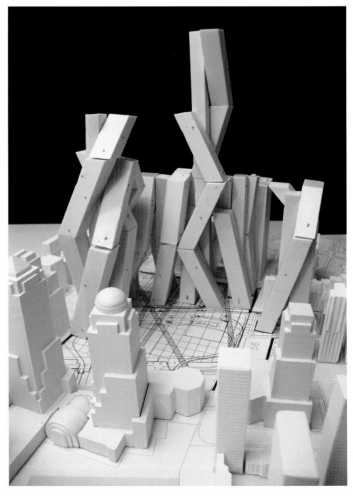

1,620 ft. (494 m)

CLOCKWISE FROM UPPER LEFT: Views from Dey,
Cortland, Fulton, and Liberty streets

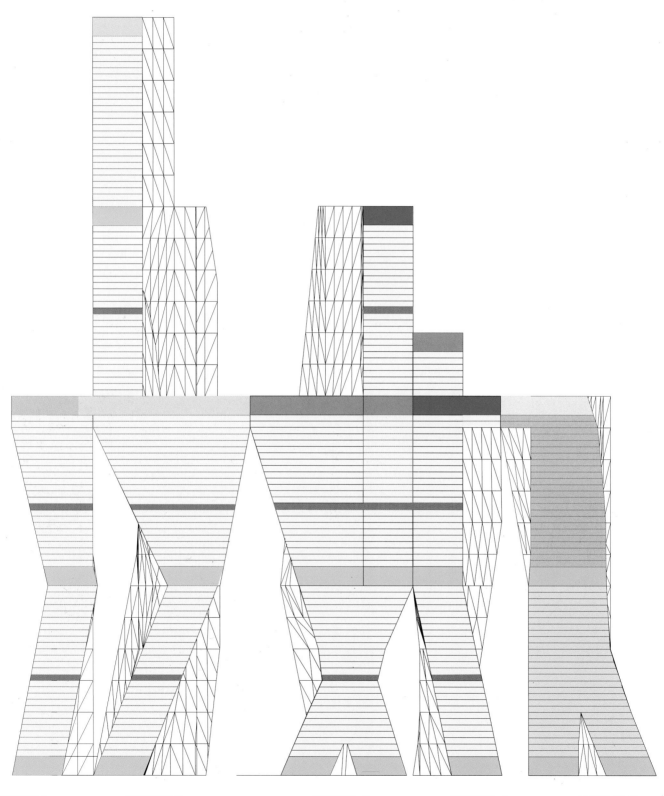

TOWER 1
1,456.280 MILLION SF

TOWER 2
3,307.182 MILLION SF

TOWER 3
2,817.490 MILLION SF

TOWER 4
1,583.722 MILLION SF

TOWER 5
1,515.720 MILLION SF

Detail of sky lobby (computer-generated image)

1,620 ft. (494 m)

Model

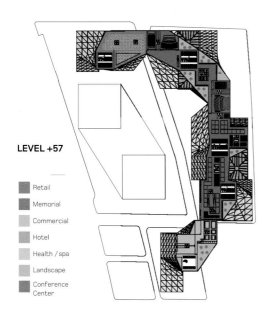

Plan, floor 57

LEVEL +57

- Retail
- Memorial
- Commercial
- Hotel
- Health /spa
- Landscape
- Conference Center

Plan, floor 14

LEVEL +14

- Retail
- Circulation
- Memorial
- Commercial
- Hotel

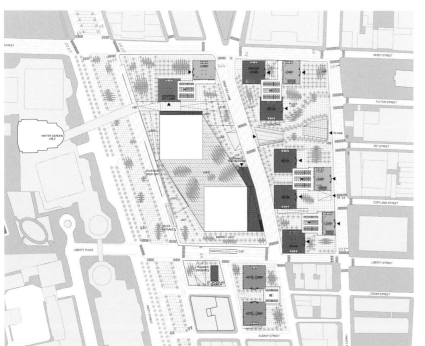

Site plan and ground-floor plans

LEVEL GRADE

- Retail
- Circulation
- Memorial
- Commercial
- Hotel

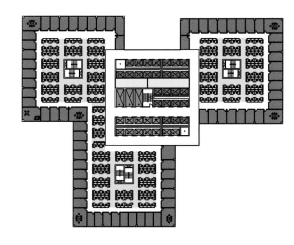

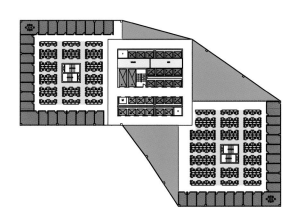

Typical floor plans, Tower 3

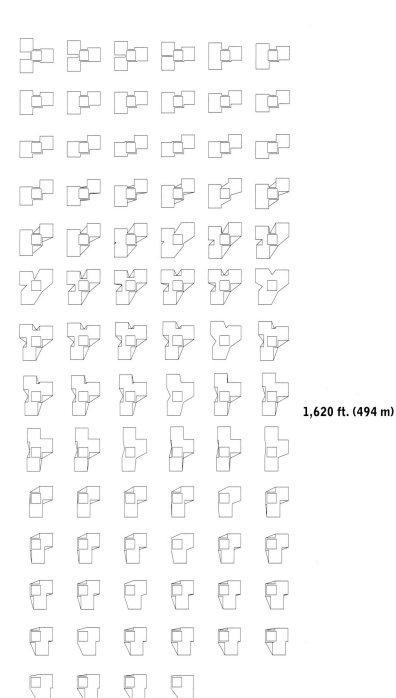

1,620 ft. (494 m)

Tower 3 floor plans

Circulation sketch, by Greg Lynn

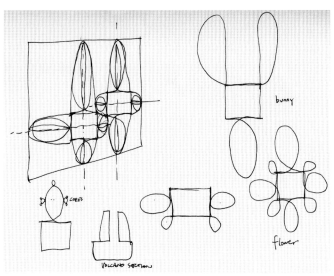

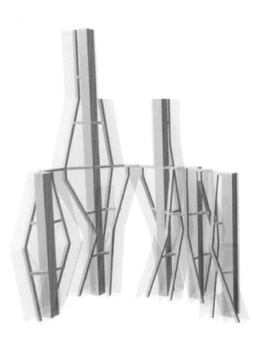

Diagram of cores and escape routes

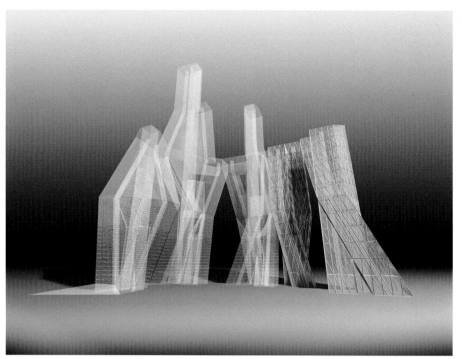

Bundled tube diagram

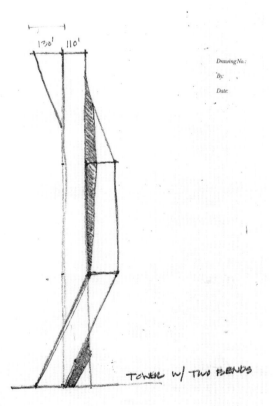

Sketch of bundled tubes, by Kevin Kennon

TOWER W/ TWO BENDS

View of towers from below
(computer-generated image)

1,620 ft. (494 m)

View from southwest (computer-generated image)

World Trade Center

New York, New York
Project, 2002

Architect: Norman Foster | Foster and Partners
Engineers: Ysrael Seinuk, Ahmad Rahimian | Cantor Seinuk Group

1,764 FEET (538 METERS) HIGH

The proposal by Foster and Partners for the World Trade Center site is a highly sophisticated and urbane integration of commercial development and transportation infrastructure, incorporating the difficult spiritual and environmental challenges of the site. The strength of the proposal is, above all, its relentless pursuit of integration. The environmental system for the site and the proposed auxiliary buildings combine elements of Foster's pioneering work in the area of obtaining energy and resource conservation through heat recovery systems at all scales. The structure of the "twinned towers" is equally progressive. These towers act jointly to resist wind loads and to allow multiple routes of circulation and egress at the midway "kissing" points and at the tops of the towers.

The structure consists of a continuous concrete core, triangular-shaped in places, with walls varying from four- to two-feet thick at the top. The perimeter is a "diagrid" of composite steel and concrete diagonal members skillfully organized in primary, secondary, and tertiary sizes, corresponding to their principal functions. Outrigger trusses link the core and the perimeter at two places. This combination of a central core and a "diagrid" structure is highly redundant and fire resistant, and answers quite clearly the natural concerns for new construction after September 11.

The form of the twinned towers is original, although consistent with Foster's continued interest in geometric inventions going back to his early collaborations with R. Buckminster Fuller. In fact, the towers bear a greater resemblance to Fuller's friend Isamu Noguchi's Akari paper lamp designs and sculptures than to conventional highrises. They have an abstract quality that is part space-age, part high modern, and are as uncommon in the New York skyline today as were the World Trade Center towers in 1973.

Foster's towers are placed on the east side of the site, across Greenwich Street from a proposed eight-acre memorial park with two "voids" over the sites of the original towers. The voids are blank walls suspended around an empty court so that from inside one can only see the sky and from outside one cannot see in. Beneath this park, and accessible by means of a grand entry space off Church Street, is a vast transportation interchange for buses, PATH trains, subways, and a proposed rail link.

The proposal is an astonishing mixture of abstraction and populism. It is unabashedly progressive in tone and substance. Like the original World Trade Center towers, it shares a kinship to the absolute optimism and professionalism of the space programs of the 1960s.

—Guy Nordenson

View from Brooklyn, looking west
across the East River

1,764 ft. (538 m)

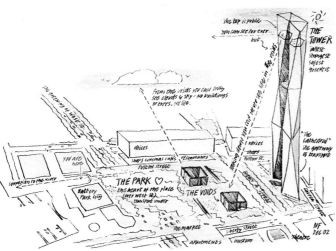

Sketch

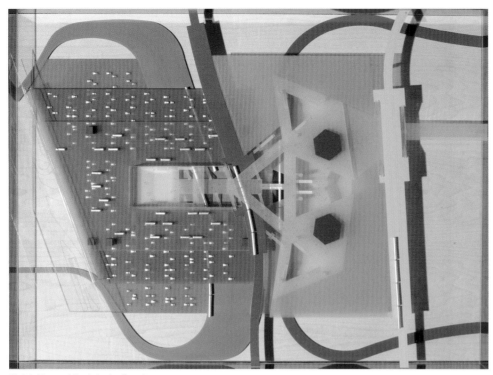

Model of transportation hub, view from above

Perspective of transportation hub
(computer-generated image)

Site plan

View looking east across the Hudson River

Typical floor plans

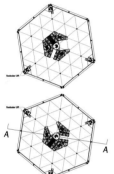

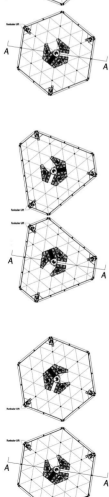

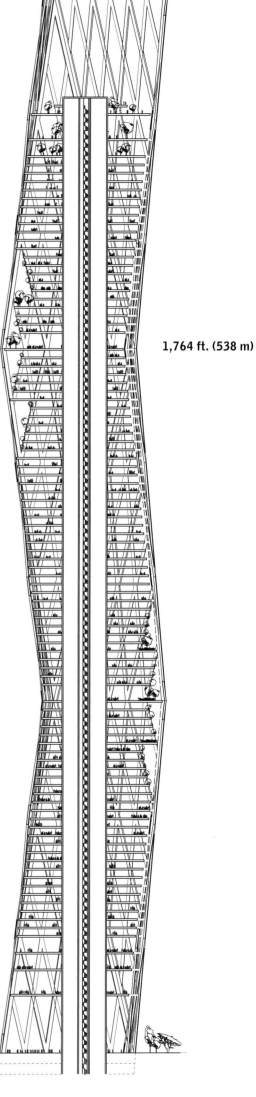

1,764 ft. (538 m)

Section

Diagrams of structural core and "diagrid" structure

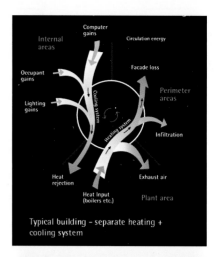

Typical building – separate heating + cooling system

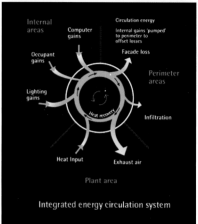

Integrated energy circulation system

Heating and cooling system diagrams, showing typical
building (TOP) and proposed integrated system (BOTTOM)

Safety diagram

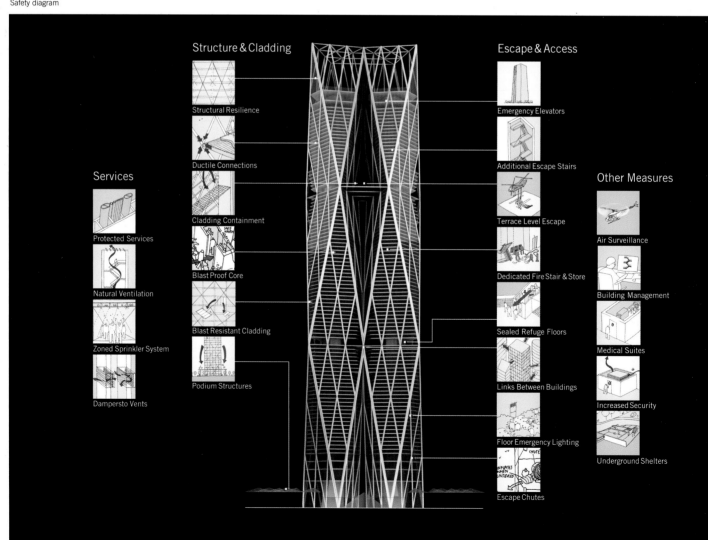

Services

Protected Services

Natural Ventilation

Zoned Sprinkler System

Dampersto Vents

Structure & Cladding

Structural Resilience

Ductile Connections

Cladding Containment

Blast Proof Core

Blast Resistant Cladding

Podium Structures

Escape & Access

Emergency Elevators

Additional Escape Stairs

Terrace Level Escape

Dedicated Fire Stair & Store

Sealed Refuge Floors

Links Between Buildings

Floor Emergency Lighting

Escape Chutes

Other Measures

Air Surveillance

Building Management

Medical Suites

Increased Security

Underground Shelters

View looking south

1,764 ft. (538 m)

Sustainability diagram

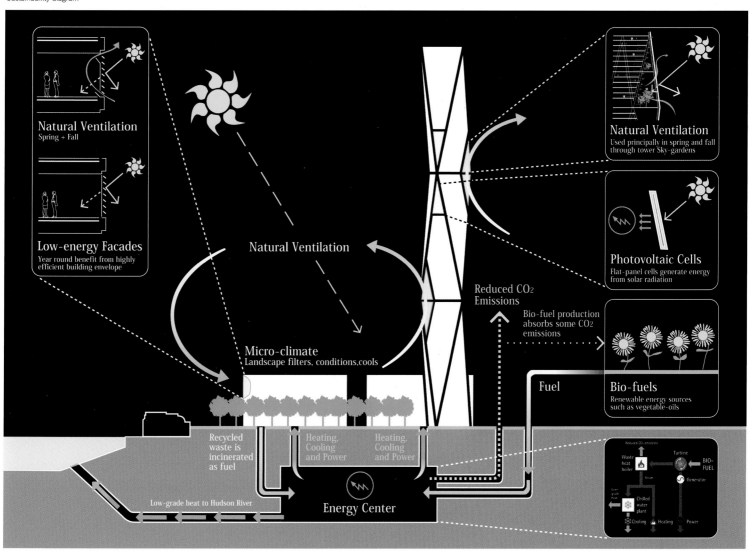

Natural Ventilation
Spring + Fall

Low-energy Facades
Year round benefit from highly
efficient building envelope

Natural Ventilation

Micro-climate
Landscape filters, conditions,cools

Recycled
waste is
incinerated
as fuel

Low-grade heat to Hudson River

Heating,
Cooling
and Power

Heating,
Cooling
and Power

Energy Center

Natural Ventilation
Used principally in spring and fall
through tower Sky-gardens

Photovoltaic Cells
Flat-panel cells generate energy
from solar radiation

Reduced CO2
Emissions

Bio-fuel production
absorbs some CO2
emissions

Fuel

Bio-fuels
Renewable energy sources
such as vegetable-oils

7 South Dearborn

Chicago, Illinois
Project, 1998

Architect: Adrian D. Smith | Skidmore, Owings & Merrill
Engineer: William F. Baker | Skidmore, Owings & Merrill

2,000 FEET (610 METERS) HIGH

This project, designed by Adrian D. Smith and William F. Baker of Skidmore, Owings & Merrill, Chicago, would now be the tallest structure in the world, at 108 stories, had it been built. Surpassing the CN Tower in Toronto by 234 feet (1976), it would also stand well above the Sears Tower (1974), the Hancock tower (1976), and the Aon (formerly Standard Oil of Indiana) Tower in Chicago (1973), a worthy successor to the many years of innovative Chicago skyscrapers.

The site is in downtown Chicago on the southeast corner of Dearborn and Madison streets. The building as designed occupies less than a third of a block, with a setback of only ten feet from the property line. The design is straightforward and functional. A central sixty-seven-foot-square hollow mast of reinforced concrete rises from a foundation of straight-shaft caissons all the way to the base of the antennae. The building envelope tapers upwards from the 185-square-foot parking and office levels in twenty-foot increments four times over the height of the whole. The first forty-eight floors are devoted to parking and office space. Above the fifty-fifth floor are three twenty-story blocks, two of which are residential and one, at the top, dedicated to broadcasting equipment. These blocks are cantilevered around the concrete mast and are separated by notches that cut back to the face of the mast.

The notches reduce the building's wind-related vibrations by creating local turbulence that impedes the formation and shedding of wind vortices. Vortex formation and shedding are the principal causes of high-wind building vibrations that disturb occupants. With apartments located 1,000 feet high this is a key concern. The Skidmore, Owings & Merrill design also includes a tuned liquid column damper at the top to help further decrease these vibrations.

The structure itself is designed as a stayed mast, coupling the concrete core and eight mega-columns aligned with the core walls with fifty-five-foot-tall outrigger trusses located at the fiftieth floor. The mega-columns anchor into a perimeter well around the lower parking levels, which serves as a stiff base. Because of the notches there is no outrigger at the top of the core, since no stays can run continuously.

There are separate elevators for low- and high-rise offices (eight and six, respectively) and the residential floors (a total of five), all contained in the concrete core. Four mechanical floors service the different program spaces.

The building continues the Chicago tradition of placing high-rise residences over office space. It rises in an absolute line perpendicular to the horizon of the Great Plains and Lake Michigan. The view from the apartments over the wide extension of the Jeffersonian grid is unmatched.

With the clarity and innovation of its program—a thin building wrapper wound about an antenna—the building designed for 7 South Dearborn is a direct descendent of the rigorous functionalism of the Chicago School. It also succeeds, to use the literary scholar Harold Bloom's phrase, in opening a "clear imaginative space" around it.
—Guy Nordenson

TOP Diagram of wind eddies
BOTTOM Diagram of aerodynamics
OPPOSITE Model

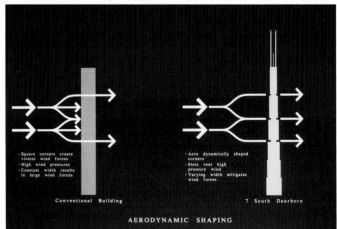

2,000 ft. (610 m)

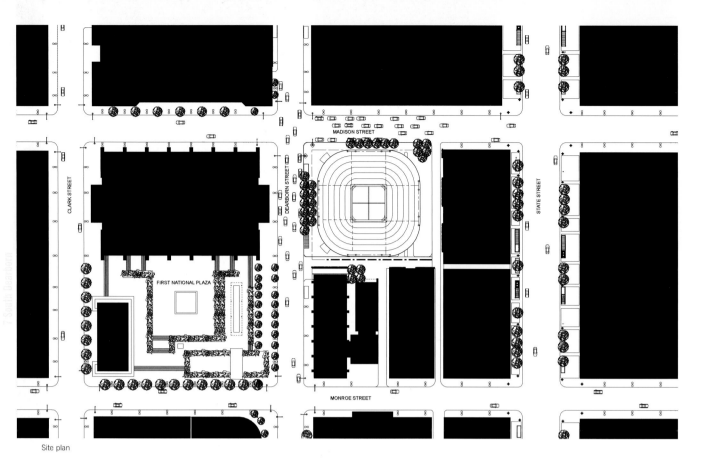

Site plan

Axonometric view of model

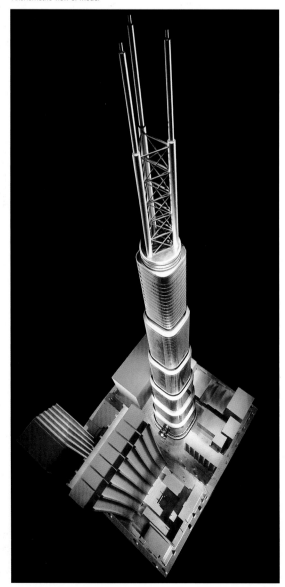

Typical plan, tier 3

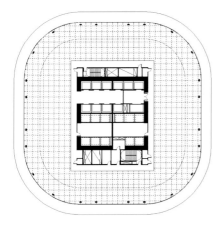

Typical office plan, tier 2

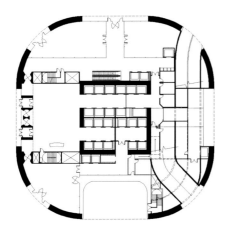

Ground-floor plan

Section

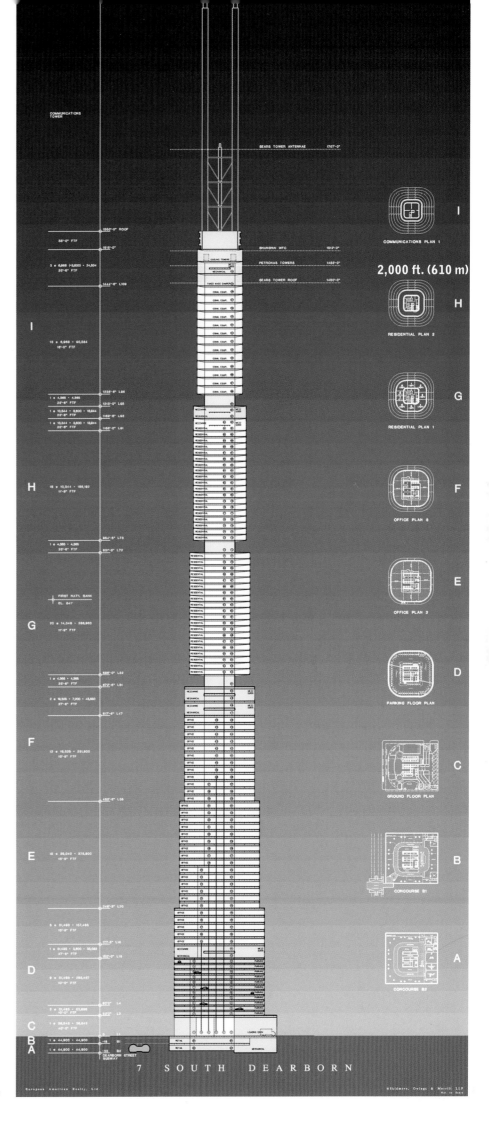

7 SOUTH DEARBORN

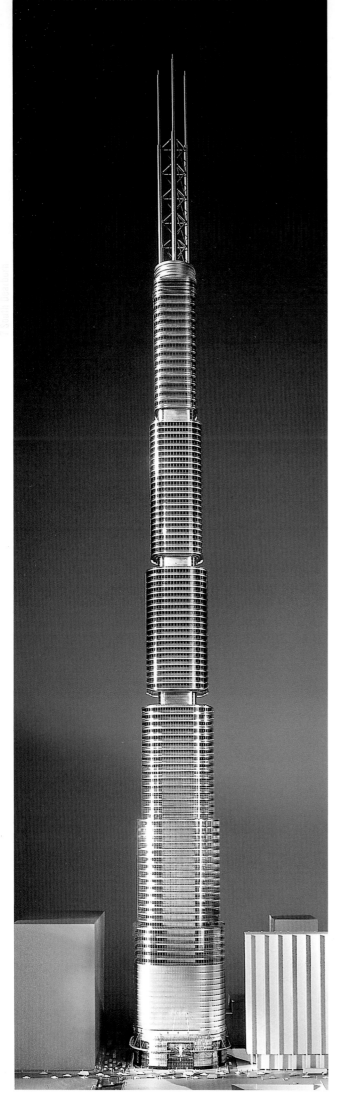

Building and site models in the wind tunnel

Model

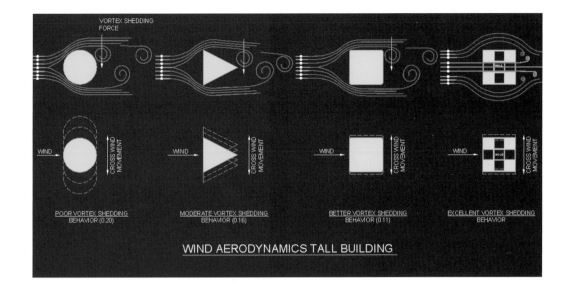

Diagrams of building aerodynamics

VORTEX SHEDDING FORCE

WIND | CROSS WIND MOVEMENT

POOR VORTEX SHEDDING BEHAVIOR (0.20)

WIND | CROSS WIND MOVEMENT

MODERATE VORTEX SHEDDING BEHAVIOR (0.16)

WIND | CROSS WIND MOVEMENT

BETTER VORTEX SHEDDING BEHAVIOR (0.11)

WIND | HOLE | CROSS WIND MOVEMENT

EXCELLENT VORTEX SHEDDING BEHAVIOR

WIND AERODYNAMICS TALL BUILDING

2,000 ft. (610 m)

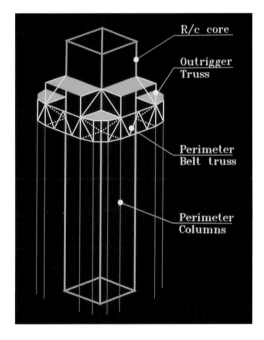

Outrigger diagram

R/c core

Outrigger Truss

Perimeter Belt truss

Perimeter Columns

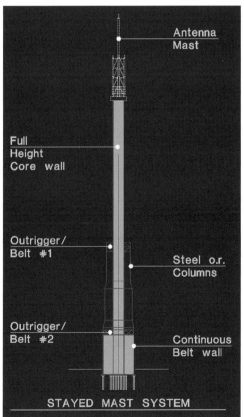

Antenna Mast

Full Height Core wall

Outrigger/ Belt #1

Steel o.r. Columns

Outrigger/ Belt #2

Continuous Belt wall

STAYED MAST SYSTEM

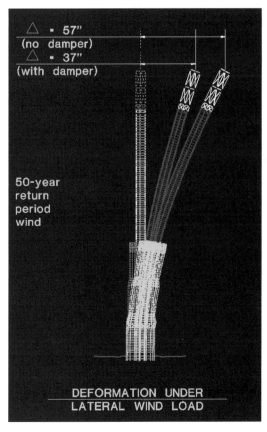

△ = 57" (no damper)
△ = 37" (with damper)

50-year return period wind

DEFORMATION UNDER LATERAL WIND LOAD

LEFT Diagram of stayed-mast system
RIGHT Diagram of wind-load deformation

Appendix

This listing provides additional data on the projects featured on pages 34–175. It is arranged according to the sequence of the plates.

Edificio Manantiales

Santiago, Chile. 1997–99

Architects: Luis Izquierdo W., Antonia Lehmann S. B., Raimundo Lira V., José Domingo Peñafiel E.

Engineer: Luis Soler P.

Height: 187 feet (57 meters)

Inhabitable floors: 17

Site dimensions: 17,869 sq. ft. (1,805 sq. m)

Gross floor area: 52,763 sq. ft. (15,989 sq. m)

Program: Office, commercial

Foundation and soil: Grid of beams and individual foundations

Floor structure: 19-cm pre-stressed slabs

Lateral system: Concrete shear-wall core and peripheral concrete frames

Principal materials: Concrete, granite, and glass

Client: Constructora Manantiales LTDA.

Developer: Martin Riesco W.

Design team: Miguel Villegas (draftsman); Juan Erenchun S. (project structural engineer); CINTEC (HVAC) (electrical engineer); Jorge Fleischman, Fleischman S.A. (project electrical engineer); Kenneth Page (project plumbing engineer); Tomás and Mario Guendelman (seismic consultants); Technal (curtain wall windows); Oriana Ponzini (lighting analysis); Teresa Moller R. (landscape architect)

Monte Laa PORR Towers

Monte Laa Development

Vienna, Austria. Design, 2000–02; projected completion, 2006

Architect: Hans Hollein I Atelier Hollein

Engineer: Joseph Janda I Projektierungsbüro für Industrie-, Hoch- und Tiefbau

Height: 361 feet (110 meters)

Inhabitable floors: 29

Site dimensions: 14,316 sq. ft. (1,330 sq. m)

Gross floor area: 343,381 sq. ft. (31,900 sq. m)

Program: Office, hotel, conference, and press center

Foundation and soil: Combined pile and slab foundation

Floor structure: Reinforced 24-cm concrete slab or 11-cm concrete slab

Lateral system: Staircase and elevator core with additional lateral brace frame according to direction; core is eccentric

Principal materials: Glass and concrete

Developer: PORR Immoprojekt GmbH

Design team: Albert Wimmer (architect); Ulf Kotz (project architect); Michael Pitsch, Alfred Strommer (project structural engineers); Erich Szczur (project mechanical engineer); Robert Bauer (project electrical engineer); Consult Plan (curtain wall); Martha Schwartz, Inc. (landscape architect)

Max Reinhardt Haus

Berlin, Germany. Project, 1992–93

Architect: Peter Eisenman I Eisenman Architects

Engineer: Edward Messina I Severud Associates

Height: 420 feet (128 meters)

Inhabitable floors: 39

Site dimensions: 56,460 sq. ft. (5,703 sq. m)

Gross floor area: 950,400 sq. ft. (96,000 sq. m)

Program: Office, hotel, theaters, retail, and fitness center

Client: Advanta Management AG

Design team: George Kewin (associate principal-in-charge); Edward Mitchell, Lindy Roy, Richard Labonte (project architects); Armand Biglari, Brad Gildea, Norbert Holthausen, Gregory Luhan, Stefania Rinaldi, David Schatzle, Jon Stephens (project team); Federico Beulcke, Mark Bretler, Andrew Burmeister, Robert Holten, Patrick Keane, Brad Khouri, Joseph Lau, Vincent LeFeuvre, Fabian Lemmel, John Maze, Steven Meyer, Debbie Park, Silke Potting, Benjamin Wade (project assistants); Fritz Neumeyer, Kurt Forster (historians); Donnell Consultants; Hanna/Olin (landscape architect)

Elephant and Castle Eco Towers

London, England. Project, 2000

Architect: Ken Yeang I T. R. Hamzah & Yeang

Engineer: Christopher McCarthy I Battle McCarthy

Height: Tower 1: 459 feet (140 meters); Tower 2: 240 feet (73 meters)

Inhabitable floors: 32

Site dimensions: 170 acres

Gross floor area: Tower 1: 276,304 sq. ft.; Tower 2: 95,765 sq. ft.

Program: Office, hotel, residential, retail, leisure, community facilities, parks

Foundation and soil: Pile foundation

Floor structure: Steel frame

Lateral system: Concrete or steel braced cores

Developer: Southwark Land Regeneration Plc

Design team: Ridzwa Fathan (design director); Portia Reynolds (design architect); Ooi Tee Lee, Loh Hock Jin, Ong Eng Huat (project team); Chong Woon Wee (project architect); Marc Lehmann, Katie Vaughan (project and senior structural engineers); Martin Fenn, Chris Dunn (structural technicians); Derek Lovejoy Partnership (landscape architect)

Electricité de France (EDF) Headquarters

La Défense, Paris, France. 1995–2002
Architect: Henry N. Cobb I Pei Cobb Freed & Partners
Engineer: Jean Heuber I SETEC
Height: 486 feet (148 meters)
Inhabitable floors: 40
Site dimensions: 3,500 sq. m
Gross floor area: 74,291 sq. m
Program: Office
Foundation and soil: 2-m concrete slab under central core;
    perimeter columns on foundation wall
Floor structure: 260-mm and 180-mm reinforced-concrete
    slab
Lateral system: Central concrete core with facade columns
    and beams
Principal materials: Steel, concrete, and glass
Developer: Hines France
Design team: Michael D. Flynn (partner for curtain
    wall/building technology); Roy G. Barris, Robert Milburn,
    Stephen Rustow, Christopher L. Olsen, Fintan Dunne,
    Michael Lyon, Daniel Silver, Euk Kwon, Daniel Cantwell,
    Christian D'Silva; J. M. Jaeger (project structural
    engineer)
Local architects: Saubot-Rouit & Associés: Jean Rouit,
    Louison Gorgiard, Sylvestre Gulacsy, Kate McGlone

Landmark Lofts

New York, New York. Project, 2001–03
Architect: Jean Nouvel I Ateliers Jean Nouvel
Height: 490 feet (149 meters)
Inhabitable floors: 33
Gross floor area: 165, 000 sq. ft. (15,300 sq. m)
Program: Residential
Client: Landmark Development
Design team: Hala Warde (project manager); Gasto Tolila,
    Antonia Pesenti, Julie Fernandez, Nicholas Gilliland;
    Etienne Follenfant (models); Nicolas Laisne (computer
    images)
Local architect: Gary Handel & Associates

Arcos Bosques Corporativo

Tower 1
Mexico City, Mexico. 1993–96
Architects: Teodoro González de Léon, J. Francisco Serrano,
    Carlos Tejeda
Engineer: Alejandro Fierro Manly I Diseño y Supervisíon
Height: 530 feet (162 meters)
Inhabitable floors: 33
Site dimensions: 186,657 sq. ft. (17,332 sq. m)
Gross floor area: 1,502,250 sq. ft. (139,588 sq. m)
Program: Office, commercial, parking
Foundation and soil: Pile foundation with tie beams on solid
    base rock
Floor structure: Waffle slabs supported on axial beams of
    reinforced concrete
Lateral system: Ductile beam-and-column frame
Principal material: Concrete
Developer: Dine S.A. de C.V.
Design team: Antonio Rodríguez Cruz, José Arce Gargollo,
    Juan Espinoza Campoverde (architects); Raymundo
    López Blas, José Luis Juárez, Roberto Morales Nava,
    Hector Chamorro, Maribel Acosta (structural engineers);
    Tecnoproyectos (electrical engineer); Garza Maldonado y
    Asociados (plumbing); Calefaccion y Ventilacion (HVAC);
    Grupo Marpe (smart system); Grupo Meta (curtain wall);
    Teodoro González De Léon, J. Francisco Serrano, Carlos
    Tejeda (landscape architects)

30 St. Mary Axe

Swiss Reinsurance Headquarters

London, England. Design, 1997–2000; projected completion, 2004

Architect: Norman Foster | Foster and Partners

Engineer: John Brazier | Ove Arup & Partners

Height: 590 feet (180 meters)

Inhabitable floors: 40

Site dimensions: 1.4 acres

Gross floor area: 693,950 sq. ft. (64,469 sq. m)

Program: Office, retail, catering

Foundation and soil: Straight-shafted concrete piles in London Clay

Floor structure: Lightweight concrete on metal deck over composite structural steel frame

Lateral system: Perimeter steel "diagrid" of inclined intersecting columns and horizontal hoops around building circumference

Principal materials: Glass, steel, and concrete

Developer: Swiss Reinsurance

Design team: Ken Shuttleworth, Robin Partington (principals); Francis Aish, Gamma Basra, Geoff Bee, Ian Bogle, Julian Cross, Joel Davenport, Ben Dobbin, Michael Gentz, Rob Harrison, Paul Kalkhoven, Chris Kallan, Jürgen Kuppers, Paul Leadbeatter, Stuart Milne, Jacob Nørlov, Tim O'Rourke, Ben Puddy, Jason Parker, Simon Reed, Narinder Sagoo, Sebastian Schoell, Michael Sehmsdorf, John Small, Robbie Turner, Neil Vandersteen, John Walden, Tim Walpole-Walsh, Hugh Whitehead, Richard Wotton, Helen Yabsley; Paul Scott (project architect); Adrian Campbell, Paul Cross, John Hirst, Dominic Munro; Hilson Moran Partnership Ltd. (mechanical engineers); BDSP Partners (environmental engineers); Emmer Pfenniger & Partner (curtain wall); Derek Lovejoy Partnership (landscape architect)

Fifth Avenue and Forty-second Street Tower

New York, New York. Project, 2002

Architect: Steven Holl, Solange Fabião | Steven Holl Architects

Engineers: Robert Silman, Nat Oppenheimer | Robert Silman Associates

Height: 585 feet (178 meters)

Inhabitable floors: 37 (36 above grade; 1 below grade)

Site dimensions: 13,355 sq. ft.

Gross floor area: 401,330 sq. ft.

Program: Office, retail, restaurant

Client: Fifth at 42nd LLC

Developer: Axel Stawski

Design team: Ziad Jamaleddine, Irene Vogt (architects); Simone Giostra (project architect); Gordon Smith (curtain wall)

New York Times Headquarters

New York, New York. Project, 2000

Architects: Frank O. Gehry | Gehry and Partners; David Childs | Skidmore, Owings & Merrill

Engineers: William F. Baker, Hal Iyengar | Skidmore, Owings & Merrill

Height: 606 feet (185 meters)

Inhabitable floors: 43

Site dimensions: 80,000 sq. ft.

Gross floor area: approx. 1,530,000 sq. ft.

Program: Office, retail

Client: The New York Times Company / Forest City Ratner Companies

Developer: Forest City Ratner Companies

Design team: Randy Jefferson, Jim Glymph (project partners); Edwin Chan (project designer); George Metzger (project architect); David Nam, Sean Gallivan, Matthew Gagnon, Ana Henton, Steffen Leisner, Christopher Deckwitz, Anand Devarajan, Jose Catriel Tulian, Michelle Kaufman, Kamran Ardalan, Cara Cragan, Chad Dyner, Sean Gale, Eric Jones, Meaghan Lloyd, Diego Petrate, Birgit Schneider, Zohar Schwartz, Brian Zamora (project team); Marilyn Taylor (urban design and planning partner), Ross B. Wimer (senior designer); T.J. Gottesdiener (managing partner); Scott Duncan, Ursula Schneider, Donald Holt, Michael Fei, Tran Vinh, Samer Bitar, Simone Pfeiffer, Dale Greenwald, Shashi Cann, Peter Buendgen, Kaz Morihata (project team)

Turning Torso

Apartment and Office Tower

Malmö, Sweden. Design 1999–2001; projected completion, 2005

Architect: Santiago Calatrava

Engineer: Santiago Calatrava

Height: 623 feet (190 meters)

Inhabitable floors: 50

Site dimensions: 2,500 sq. m

Gross floor area: 2,930,266 sq. m

Program: Office, hotel, residential

Foundation and soil: Circular flat RC slab (for structural core), anchored pile foundation (for exoskeleton)

Floor structure: Reinforced-concrete slabs (flat and conical)

Lateral system: Circular reinforced-concrete structural core; steel-truss exoskeleton

Principal materials: Concrete and steel

Developer: HSB-Malmö, Sweden, Managing Director, Johnny Örbäck

Design team: Christian Brändle (project manager); David Mizrahi, Matthias Hugi, Lorenzo Gottardi, Ivan Itschner, Fabio Guerra, Bruno Stöckenius (architects); Mario Rando, Manuel Alvarez (project structural engineer); Steve Webb, Raul Rodriguez, Fernando Ibañez, Pascal Guignard (engineers); Bent Dahlgren AB, Gothenburg, Sweden (project mechanical engineer); Santiago Calatrava (landscape architect)

Local architect: SAMARK, Arkitektur & Design AB, Malmö and Stockholm, Sweden

Industrialized Housing System

Korea. Project, 1992

Architect: Richard Rogers I Richard Rogers Partnership

Engineer: John Miles I Ove Arup & Partners

Height: 660 feet (201 meters)

Client: Hanseem Corporation

Design team: Laurie Abbott (project director); Mike Davis, Stuart Forbes, Marco Goldschmied, John Lowe, Jackie Moore, Richard Paul, Andrew Wright, John Young

22 Leadenhall Street

London, England. Project, 2002–03

Architect: Richard Rogers I Richard Rogers Partnership

Engineer: David Glover I Ove Arup & Partners

Height: 728 feet (222 meters)

Inhabitable floors: 47

Site dimensions: 3,484 sq. m

Gross floor area: 900,000 sq. ft.

Program: Office, retail

Foundation and soil: Large-diameter deep piles in London Clay.

Floor structure: Long-span lightweight steel floors with composite decking

Lateral system: Perimeter braced "megaframe" tube structure

Client: British Land Company PLC

Design team: Graham Stirk (project director); Andy Bryce, Maxine Campbell, Mark Hallett, John McElgunn, Russell Gilchrist, Louise Palomba, William Wimshurst; Damian Eley (project structural engineer), Paul Cross, Colin Jackson, Chris Neighbour, Andy Pye; Andy Sedgwick (project director, building services and project electrical engineer); Jonathan Ward (project mechanical engineer)

Central Chinese Television (CCTV) Tower

Beijing, China. Design, 2002–04; projected completion, 2008

Architects: Rem Koolhaas, Ole Scheeren | Office for Metropolitan Architecture

Engineers: Cecil Balmond, Craig Gibbons, Michael Kwok, Rory McGowan | Ove Arup & Partners

Height: 768 feet (234 meters)

Inhabitable floors: 49

Site dimensions: 264,000 sq. m (17.8 hectares)

Gross floor area: CCTV: 3,851,100 sq. ft. (389,079 sq. m); TVCC: 988,237 sq. ft. (99,822 sq. m)

Program: CCTV: Office, news and broadcasting, broadcasting and transmission, production; TVCC: Hotel, public facilities, theater, exhibition spaces

Foundation and soil: 8-m-thick slabs on 70-m piles in alluvial soil

Floor structure: Superstructure: Composite steel beam and concrete slab on steel and steel-reinforced concrete columns. Substructure: Reinforced-concrete beam and column frames with flat slabs

Lateral system: Perimeter braced structural tube

Principal structural system: Transfer trusses

Principal materials: Reinforced concrete, structural mild steel

Client: Central China Television (CCTV)

Design team: Ellen van Loon (technical advisor); Shohei Shigematsu, Dongmei Yao, Adrianne Fisher, Anu Leinonen, Charles Berman, Erez Ella, David Chacon, Hiromasa Shirai, Chris van Duin (project architects); Abhijit Kapade, Wenchian Shi, Gabriella Bojalil, Catarina Canas, Michel van der Kar, Tian-Tian Xu, Stuart Maddocks, Faustina Tsai, Gaspard Estourgie, Andre Schmidt, Torsten Schröder, Kunle Adeyemi, Cristina Murphy; Chris Carroll, Goman Ho, Alexis Lee, Stuart Smith (project structural engineers); Paul Cross, Mimmy Dino, Keita Ishimitsu, Richard Lawson, Peng Liu, Andrew Luong, John MacArthur, Jack Pappin, Dan Pook, Chas Pope, Andrew Smith, Ben Urick, Terence Yip; Alistair Guthrie (principal architect building services); Clodagh Ryan, Iain Lyall (project mechanical engineers); John Pullen, Dane Green, Kenneth Sin (project electrical engineers); David George (project plumbing engineer); William Wong, Lewis Shiu, William Zhang, Olly Base, Lesley Gale, Jodh Singh, Eddie Scuffell, Chi-Wing Chow, John Haddon, Bob Lau, Graham Humphreys, Simon Brimble, Angela Green, David Hadden, Chai-Kok eow, Dorothee Richter, David Pritchard; Front, New York (curtain wall); Dorsser Blesgraaf, Eindhoven, The Netherlands (acoustics); Duck S Scéno, Vaulx-en-Velin, France (scenography); Lerch Bates & Associates, Sheerwater, Woking, UK (vertical transportation); ECADI, Shanghai, China and Sand Brown Associates, London, UK (broadcast design); Danud Langdon & Seah, Hong Kong (cost consultants); MADA s.p.a.m., Shanghai, China (strategic advisor); DMJMH+N, Los Angeles (highrise)

Local architects and engineers: ECADI, Shanghai, China: Shen Di, Long Ge, Wang Dasui, Han Hui, Cheng Yongwei, Huang Renying (project management team); Wang Xiaoan, Li Yao, Xu Jialong (chief architects); Zhao Weiliang, Sun Yu, Ling Ji, Jia Bo, Dai Yiming, Dai Weiwei, Zhang Sheng, Xiang Ming, Wu Zheng, Fan Yifei, Xu Nuo, Guo Yuming, Chen Li; Wen Boyin, Hu Yangqi, Feng Xudong (chief engineers)

Highcliff and The Summit

Hong Kong, China. 1995–2002

Architect: Dennis Lau Wing-kwong | Dennis Lau & Ng Chun Man Architects and Engineers

Engineer: Ad Gouwerok | Magnusson Klemencic Associates

Height: Highcliff: 827 feet (252 meters); The Summit: 722 (220 meters)

Inhabitable floors: Highcliff: 71; The Summit: 56

Site dimensions: Highcliff: 4,366 sq. m; The Summit 3,045 sq. m

Gross floor area: Highcliff: 34,931 sq. m; The Summit: 15,225 sq. m

Program: Residential

Foundation and soil: Composite system of bored piles, thick mat, basement slabs, and concrete walls atop bedrock

Lateral system: Reinforced-concrete core

Developer: Highcliff: Highcliff Investment Ltd; The Summit: Hang Lung Properties

Design team: Highcliff: Joseph Tang Chun-sing (project design architect); Henry Lau King-chiu (project architect); K. Casey Caughie (structural engineering project manager); Tony Tschanz, Peter Heathcoate, Ignnasius Sellie, Adam Koczarski, Ola Johansen, Hans-Erik Blomgren, Jin Yu, Scott Erickson, Silvester Johnson; The Summit: Lee Tit-sun (project architect); Ringo Cheng Che-chung, Raphael Chong Kock-yuen, Maggie Lai; K. Casey Caughie (structural engineering project manager); Tony Tschanz, Peter Heathcoate, Mike Valley, Adam Koczarski, Ola Johansen, Dave Field, Ichiro Ikeda, Anne Gochenour; CDC Ltd (curtain wall); ADI Ltd (The Summit, landscape architect)

Local engineers: Highcliff: Canwest Consultants International Ltd.: David Yip Yun-tong (registered structural engineer); The Summit: Maunsell Structural Consultants Ltd.: David Lee Chin (registered structural engineer)

JR Ueno Railway Station Redevelopment

Ueno, Tokyo, Japan. Project, 1988–95

Architect: Arata Isozaki | Arata Isozaki & Associates

Engineer: Toshihiko Kimura | Kimura Structural Engineers

Height: 987 feet (301 meters)

Inhabitable floors: 63

Gross floor area: 260,000 sq. m

Program: Hotel, retail, theater, art gallery, railway station

Principal structural system: Reinforced concrete; steel construction

Client: East Japan Railway Company

Design team: Shuichi Fujle (project manager); Kenji Sato (project architect); Naoki Ogawa, Yasuyuki Watanabe, Jun Aiba, Joachim Frey, Andrea Hold, Shoji Ishiguro (model maker); Kankyo Engineering Inc. (mechanical engineers); Akeno Sanitary Engineering Consultants (fire prevention)

London Bridge Tower

London, England. Design, 2000–03; projected completion, 2009

Architect: Renzo Piano | Renzo Piano Building Workshop

Engineer: Paul Nuttall | Ove Arup & Partners

Height: 1,016 feet (310 meters)

Inhabitable floors: 68 (65 above grade; 3 below grade)

Site dimensions: 46,800 sq. ft. (4,345 sq. m)

Gross floor area: 1,340,000 sq. ft. (125,000 sq. m)

Program: Office, hotel, residential, public amenities

Foundation and soil: Straight shafted bored piles in Thames sand

Floor structure: Basement: concrete slabs; Office floors: lightweight concrete slab on profiled metal decking on steel beams; Hotel and residential floors: cranked steel beams carrying profiled composite slabs or post-tensioned reinforced concrete flat slab

Lateral system: Central core and outrigger at mid-height

Developer: Sellar Property Group

World Trade Center

New York, New York. Project, 2002

Architects: Richard Meier | Richard Meier & Partners Architects; Peter Eisenman | Eisenman Architects; Charles Gwathmey | Gwathmey Siegel & Associates; Steven Holl | Steven Holl Architects

Engineer: Craig Schwitters | Buro Happold

Height: 1,111 feet (337 meters)

Inhabitable floors: 74

Site dimensions: Approx. 30 acres

Gross floor area: 8,591,250 sq. ft.

Program: Office, mechanical, hotel, cultural facilities, convention center and meeting rooms, restaurants, and lobbies

Lateral system: Braced frames in the short direction; internal concrete shear walls at elevators and service cores in the long direction

Principal structural system: Continuous super-floors, reinforced-concrete shear-wall cores, and composite concrete perimeter columns

Principal materials: Steel and reinforced concrete

Client: Lower Manhattan Development Corporation

Design team: Richard Meier & Partners Architects: Lisetta Koe, Alfonso D'Onofrio, Michael Gruber, Milton Lam, Michal Taranto, Elizabeth Lee, Esther Kim, Tetsuhito Abe; Eisenman Architects: Cynthia Davidson, Pablo Lorenzo-Eiroa, Marta Caldeira, Selim Vural, Milisani Mniki, Larissa Babij; Gwathmey Siegel & Associates: Robert Siegel, Gerald Gendreau, Scott Skipworth, Brian Arnold, Shannon Walsh, Laurel Kolsby, Yongseok John, Tim Butler, Clarisse Labro, Barry Yanku; Steven Holl Architects: Makram el Kadi, Simone Giostra, Christian Wassmann, Irene Vogt; Olin Partnership: Laurie Olin; Arup Services Ltd.: Greg Hodkinson, Thomas McGuire, Michael O'Neill, Simon Rule; Buro Happold: Paul Wesbury, Greg Otto, Peter Chipchase; Mike Rushman (land strategies)

New York Times Headquarters

New York, New York. Design, 2000–03; projected completion, 2006

Architect: Renzo Piano I Renzo Piano Building Workshop

Engineer: Thomas Scarangello I Thornton-Tomasetti Engineers

Height: 1,140 feet (348 meters)

Inhabitable floors: 50

Site dimensions: 80,000 sq. ft.

Gross floor area: 1,546,625 sq. ft.

Program: Office, retail

Foundation system and soil type: Spread footings on bedrock

Floor structure: Concrete slab on composite metal deck supported by composite steel beams and girders

Lateral system: braced core and four exterior braced X-frames

Principal materials: Steel, concrete, and glass

Client: New York Times Company / Forest City Ratner Companies

Developer: Forest City Ratner Companies

Design team: Leonard M. Joseph, Aine M. Brazil, Kyle E. Krall, Erleen K. Hatfield, Erin O'Neil, Cindy Xin Zheng, Jefferey A. Callow (structural engineering); Heitmann & Associates, Inc. (curtain wall); H. M. White Site Architects (landscape architect)

Local architect: Fox and Fowle Architects, P.C. (executive architect)

Jin Mao Tower

Pudong New Area, Shanghai, China. 1993–99

Architect: Adrian D. Smith I Skidmore, Owings & Merrill

Engineer: D. Stanton Korista I Skidmore, Owings & Merrill

Height: 1,380 feet (421 meters)

Inhabitable floors: 86

Site dimensions: 2.36 hectares

Gross floor area: 2,627,163 sq. ft. (265,370 sq. m)

Program: Office, hotel, retail, parking, and mechanical

Foundation and soil: 280 ft. long, high-capacity steel-tube piles down to dense sand strata

Floor structure: Compact structural steel beams and compact metal deck slab

Lateral system: Compact system of central core wall interlinked to eight mega-columns

Principal materials: Concrete and steel

Developer: China Shanghai Foreign Trade Centre Co. Ltd.

Design team: Thomas Fridstein (managing partner); Scott Timcoe, Thomas Scheckelhoff, Paul DeVylder (project managers); Steve Hubbard (senior designer); Peter Weismantle (senior technical coordinator); Louis Oswald (project technical coordinator); Nada Andric (interior designer); Mark Sarkisian (project structural engineer); Ahmad Abdelrazaq; Raymond J. Clark (principal service engineer, MEP partner); Sherman Leong (project mechanical engineer); Gil Di Iorio (senior mechanical engineer); Paul Kwong (project electrical engineer); Joe Jamal (senior electrical engineer); Robert Blohm (project plumbing engineer)

Local architects: Shanghai Institute of Design and Research (pre-construction); East China Architectural and Design Institute (construction)

Togok (XL Towers)

Seoul, Korea. Project, 1996ñ2002

Architect: Rem Koolhaas I Office for Metropolitan Architecture

Engineers: Cecil Balmond, Philip Dilley I Ove Arup & Partners

Height: 1,444 feet (440 meters)

Inhabitable floors: 103

Gross floor area: Approx. 8.2 million sq. ft.

Program: Offices, retail, hotel, residential, convention center, fusion hall, recreation and sports, virtual entertainment, mind/body temple, station

Client: Samsung Corporation

Design team: Gary Bates, Sarah Dunn, Frans Blok, Wilfried Hackenbroich, Xavier Calderon, Domenico Raimondo, Gro Bonesmo, Floris Alkemade, Mike Magner, Thorsten Deckler, Minsuk Cho, Kohei Kashimoto, Oleg Nikolaeuski; Parthesius de Rijk: Vincent de Rijk and Bert Simons (models)

Kowloon Station Tower

Kowloon, Hong Kong, China. Design, 2000–03; projected
completion, 2007
Architect: William Pedersen | Kohn Pedersen Fox Associates
Engineer: George Chan | Ove Arup & Partners; Leslie
Robertson | LERA
Height: 1,583 feet (475 meters)
Inhabitable floors: 97
Site dimensions: 98,000 sq. ft.
Gross floor area: 3,440,000 sq. ft.
Program: Office, hotel, observation deck, gym, conference
rooms, restaurant
Lateral system: Mast and outrigger
Client: Harbour Vantage Management Ltd. (A subsidiary of
Sun Hung Kai Properties Ltd.)
Design team: Paul Katz (managing principal); Andreas Hausler
(project manager); Eric Howler, Trent Tesch (senior
designers); Ernesto Trindade, Yin The, Bruno Caballe-
Munhill, Michael Arad, Gene Miao, Ignacio Iratchet,
Glen Dacosta; Alt, Phillipines (curtain wall); Belt Collins,
Hong Kong (landscape architect)
Local architect: Wong & Ouygang

World Trade Center

New York, New York. Project, 2002
Architects: United Architects: Ben van Berkel, Caroline Bos |
Un Studio; Peter Frankfurt, Mikon van Gastel | Imaginary
Forces; Kevin Kennon | Kevin Kennon Architects; Greg
Lynn | Greg Lynn FORM; Farshid Moussavi, Alejandro
Zaero-Polo | Foreign Office Architects; Jesse Reiser,
Nanako Umemoto | Reiser + Umemoto
Engineers: Aine M. Brazil, Thomas Scarangello | Thornton-
Tomasetti; Rory McGowan | Ove Arup & Partners
Height: 1,620 feet (494 meters)
Inhabitable floors: Tower 1: 55; Tower 2: 112; Tower 3: 81;
Tower 4: 65; Tower 5: 57; Total: 370
Site dimensions: Approx. 30 acres
Program: Office, hotel, residential, memorial garden,
conference center, observation deck, retail/food court,
restaurant, broadcast center
Foundation and soil: Spread footings on rock with rock
anchors
Floor structure: Slab-on-metal deck supported on composite
Lateral system: Steel beam and girder framing, concrete shear
wall core, and "diagrid" steel exoskeleton
Client: Lower Manhattan Development Corporation and Port
Authority of NY and NJ
Design team: Foreign Office Architects: Nerea Calvillo, Daniel
Lopez-Perez, Frederich Ludewig; Greg Lynn FORM:
Jacklilin Hah, Elena Manferdini, Patrick McEneany,
Florencia Pita, Rafael Cardenas, Jason de Boer, Lukas
Haller, Amanda Salud-Gallivan, Richard Weinstein (urban
design consultant); Imaginary Forces: Brian Loube, Chip
Houghton, Eric Mauer, Tali Krakowsky, Raji
Krishnaswami, Peter Cho, Kim Lilly; Kevin Kennon
Architects: Pablo Jendretzki, Gisela Vidalle, Veronica
Zalcberg, Kathleen Chia, Jennifer Cramm, Adam
Augenblick, Robert Putnam, Lewis Feldstein; Reiser +
Umemoto: Rhett Russo, Eva Perez de Vega Steele,
Wolfgang Gollwitzer, Jason Scroggin, Stephan Vary, Josh
McKeown, Akari Takebayashi, Kenji Nonobe, Hidekazu
Ota, Akira Nakamura; UN Studio: Tobias Wallisser, Astrid
Piber, Olaf Gipser, Matthew Johnston, Cynthia Markhoff,
Holger Hoffmann, Machteld Kors; Thornton-Tomasetti:
Gary Panariello, P.E., Richard Tomasetti, Daniel Cuoco,
Joseph Burns, Leonid Zborovsky; Ove Arup & Partners:
Charles Walker, Hilliary Cobo, Mahadev Raman, Nigel
Nicholls, Lip Chiong; Edwards and Kelsey Engineers
Inc.: John Pavlovich; Walker Parking: Steve Cebra; Van
Deusen Associates: Hakan Tanyeri; Thornton-Tomasetti
and Ove Arup & Partners (curtain wall); Edward and
Kelsey Engineers Inc., Walker Parking (transportation)

World Trade Center

New York, New York. Project, 2002

Architect: Norman Foster | Foster and Partners

Engineers: Ysrael Seinuk, Ahmad Rahimian | Cantor Seinuk Group

Height: 1,764 feet (538 meters)

Inhabitable floors: 98

Site dimensions: Approx. 30 acres

Gross floor area: 17,584,927 sq. ft.

Program: Office, hotel, international conference center, residential, retail, museum, theater, memorial, visitors center, transportation Interchange, sky lobbies/observation and roof terraces), services

Client: Lower Manhattan Development Corporation

Design team: Ken Shuttleworth, Spencer de Grey, Graham Phillips, Brandon Haw, Stefan Behling, Paul Scott, Tom Politowicz, Sean Affleck, Narinder Sagoo, Mark Atkinson, Stefan Abidin, Marcos de Andres, Yoon Choi, Alan Chung, Ramses Frederickx, Neryhs Phillips, David Picazo, Xavier de Kestelier, Jeremy Kim, Richard Kulczak, Anthony Lester, Agustina Rivi, Pearl Tang, James Thomas, Alex Thomson, Damian Timlin, Carsten Vollmer, William Walshe, Neil Vandersteen, Chris Windsor, John Walden, Matt Clarke, Bryan Corry, John Dixon, Joe Preston, Werner Sigg, Robert Starsmore, Diane Teague, Robert Turner, Richard Wotton, Gareth Verbiel, Hugh Whitehead, Judit Kimpian, Gerard Forde, Katy Harris, Gamma Basra, Kevin Hay; Anish Kapoor (sculptor); Roger Preston & Partners, London (environmental engineer); Space Syntax, London (pedestrian movement analysis)

7 South Dearborn

Chicago, Illinois. Project, 1998

Architect: Adrian D. Smith | Skidmore, Owings & Merrill

Engineer: William F. Baker | Skidmore, Owings & Merrill

Height: 2,000 feet (610 meters)

Inhabitable floors: 118

Site dimensions: 41,850 sq. ft.

Gross floor area: 2,006,000 sq. ft

Program: Office, residential, communications facilities, retail

Foundation and soil: Reinforced- concrete caissons into bedrock limestone

Floor structure: Office/parking: composite steel framing and metal deck slab; Residential: post-tensioned concrete beams and reinforced-concrete slabs

Lateral system: Central reinforced-concrete core linked through outrigger trusses to exterior column/wall system

Principal materials: Concrete and structural steel

Client: European American Realty, Ltd.

Design team: Richard F. Tomlinson II (managing partner); Raymond J. Clark (MEP partner);

Robert Pigati (project manager); Richard Smits (senior technical coordinator); Gil Dilorio (senior MEP engineer); Robert C. Sinn (senior and project structural engineer); Steven Hubbard (studio head and project architect); Dennis Rehill, Hun Sang, Mark Pearson (project architects); D. Stanton Korista (project structural engineer); Raymond J. Clark and Gil Dilorio (project mechanical, electrical and plumbing engineers); Horvath Reich CDC, Inc. (curtain wall); RWDI (wind tunnel)

Acknowledgments

Without the extraordinary technical, urban and aesthetic contributions of the architects and engineers represented in this volume, there would be no reason for the enormous effort that goes into getting a publication such as this into print, or the exhibition it accompanies presented to the public. In an age that favors specialization over breadth of vision, and risk aversion over thoughtful experimentation, the work of the design professionals presented here is an outstanding achievement.

Accomplishments such as these are dependent on not only strong design leadership but amazingly complex teams of professionals whose work we recognize on pages 34 to 175. The execution of such visionary projects is itself a marvel, and the builders who undertake them, as well as the clients who back them, should be recognized for their accomplishments, especially among their more conventional peers.

In a direct and very practical way, we are also grateful to the coordinators in the various offices of the architects and engineers, who provided all of the images and information, and whose dedication enabled us to incorporate the most current, up-to-the-minute material.

It was a particular pleasure to discuss this exhibition and publication with Guy Nordenson early on in the process and then have him join me as a co-curator in developing the projects and themes represented here. His insight, thoughtfulness, knowledge of the discourse between structural engineering and architecture, and belief in the spirit and civil nature of architecture is evident in the marvelous essay he has contributed to this volume. His assistant Meredith L. Bostwick provided invaluable research in surveying and categorizing tall buildings around the world, built or unbuilt since 1988, as did Derek Chan, who assisted with the background research and collection of illustrations for the essay.

Harriet Schoenholz Bee, Editorial Director of The Museum of Modern Art's Department of Publications, edited the manuscript with her characteristic care and thoroughness; her role as a thoughtful guide, critic, and advisor was, as always, invaluable. Christopher Zichello, Production Manager, oversaw its production with his keen eye, customary sense of perfection and rigor, and patience, to accommodate and integrate what seemed to be an endless list of changes. In brief, the entire book rises to the high level of quality set by the Museum's publications department, ably led by Michael Maegraith.

The distinct appearance and structural coherence of the book is due to the efforts of Catarina Tsang and Patrick Seymour. As designers with many skills, Tsang-Seymour's sensitivity ensured a compelling design that reflects the essence of tall buildings, seen throughout the book as they climb upward against backgrounds of sky blue.

The publication of this book represents the critical efforts of many people in The Museum of Modern Art's Department of Architecture and Design, all of whom bring academic credentials as well as personal commitment to their work. Tina di Carlo, Curatorial Assistant, and Bevin Cline, Assistant Curator, contributed thoughtfully written and well-researched texts for the projects. Rachel Judlowe, Coordinator, provided a much-needed sense of the project's needs and priorities within the department's overall program. All of us are indebted to her for her judicious sense of balance on the one hand and her unwavering support on the other.

Tina di Carlo also served as a very able curatorial assistant on the project from its inception. The arduous task of transforming free-form conversations, snippets of information, and murky images into solid research, reliable documents, and publication-quality artwork is a huge accomplishment. We are further grateful for her collegial manner and the thoughtful insights she always brought to her work. Intern Kevin McAlarnen conscientiously assisted in our efforts on myriad details of the publication, and Melanie Domino also provided assistance in getting the book into print.

As one of the Museum's six curatorial departments, Architecture and Design is particularly grateful for the support, financial as well as personal, it receives from its Trustee Committee, chaired by Patricia Phelps de Cisneros, and from vice chairs Barbara Jakobson and Rob Beyer.

I would also like to thank Glenn D. Lowry, Director of The Museum of Modern Art, for his steadfast support of this project—both the catalogue and the forthcoming exhibition. Regrettably, it is not possible to thank in advance the many talented and dedicated professionals on the Museum's staff who will over the coming months make the exhibition a reality. However, it is possible to predict that they, along with the senior staff of the Museum, will perform their tasks with the incredible skill and devotion for which they are so justly well known throughout the museum world. No Museum of Modern Art exhibition would be a success with the efforts of many departments, including Exhibition Design and Production, Education, Registrar, Exhibitions, Conservation, Digital Media, Graphics, and General Counsel.

This catalogue accompanies the second in a series of exhibitions on contemporary design sponsored through the generosity of Alexandra Herzan in honor of her mother, Lily Auchincloss, who for many years was a devoted supporter of the Department of Architecture and Design. For their unwavering dedication to the arts of design and the Museum's pursuit of related programs we are continually grateful.

Both catalogues in the Auchincloss series have been made possible by Elise Jaffe and Jeffery Brown's generous support. While they have provided critical assistance for many of the Department of Architecture and Design's programs, their ongoing support for its publications is deeply appreciated.

Terence Riley

Photograph Credits